T0128103

The Willing to Buy Coach

by

Dan Schultheis

and

Phil Perkins

Cover and book interior design
and financial perspective
by Sandra Dube

Copy editing by Bethany Halle

authorHOUSE®

AuthorHouse™
1663 Liberty Drive
Bloomington, IN 47403
www.authorhouse.com
Phone: 1 (800) 839-8640

Published by AuthorHouse 04/11/2018

ISBN: 978-1-5462-3639-9 (sc)
ISBN: 978-1-5462-3637-5 (hc)
ISBN: 978-1-5462-3638-2 (e)

Library of Congress Control Number: 2018904054

Print information available on the last page.

Any people depicted in stock imagery provided by Getty Images are models, and such images are being used for illustrative purposes only. Certain stock imagery © *Getty Images.*

This book is printed on acid-free paper.

Contents

About the Authors

Dan Schultheis is a speaking professional and personal coach who presents powerful and entertaining programs in the areas of business, sales and personal motivation. He brings over two decades of leadership experience in the sales and marketing of technology & service solutions. Schultheis served as CEO for Gyrus Systems, a high-tech software publishing firm headquartered in Richmond, Virginia.

Schultheis spent 25 years of his working career at IBM. His tenure there spanned a variety of positions including that of Virginia General Manager. In 1992, Schultheis founded, Personal Communications Consultants, a company that develops, promotes, and facilitates seminars, workshops, and professional development training for organizations, small groups, and individuals. Sales Mechanics is the sales consulting arm of that company.

For over 15 years, He was a Trustee for Virginia Union University, as well as a member of the James Madison University Business School Executive Advisory Council.

He has been a member of the National Speakers Association for over 10 years. He lives in Midlothian, Virginia with Carol, his wife of 49 years.

Phil Perkins is President and CEO of ACUMEN Corporation, an international supply chain and ERP consulting firm based in Richmond, Virginia. He is also the founder and principal consultant of Strategy Island, an executive peer consortium promoting life-long learning. Perkins is a noted speaker and author whose approach to managerial and industrial productivity is considered refreshing and innovative.

During his successful career he has been a technology manager in the Fortune 500 environment, a systems designer, independent consultant and ground breaking CEO. Perkins is a frequent contributor to the international conference of APICS, The Educational Society for Resource Management and is a founding member of the Institute for Enterprise-wide Solutions at Virginia Commonwealth University. In addition, he has taught management courses at the University of Richmond Management Center and is a member of an international think tank on best practices.

He has written for or been quoted in several business publications including **Inc.** magazine and his first book, ***Points of Productivity; Turning Corporate Pain to Gain***, was published in 2003. The second edition will be released later this year.

Mr. Perkins is a resident of Richmond, Virginia and Hilton Head Island, South Carolina where he and his wife are active in community affairs.

<u>Willing to Excel</u>

Here are two quick facts about the authors and their sales acumen.

> Dan Schultheis took over an under achieving IBM branch and increased revenues from $60 million to $130 million in 3 years.

> Phil Perkins revived a 'lost' deal in competition with a big six firm and major global hardware/software manufacturer to drive total billings exceeding $7 million.

"Willing To Buy" Coach

*A Management Guide to building WTB
skills in your Sales Team*

Preface

This publication is meant to be a companion piece for the book **""Willing To Buy"; A Questioning Framework for Effective Closing"** published in 2015. We sincerely hope that you read our first book and have bought this follow-up out of enthusiasm for the thoughts and ideas contained therein. But alas, we cannot make that assumption. Therefore, we want to spend a few pages defining what we call the four "pillars" that make up our tried and true framework for closing more business. These definitions come directly from the first book.

While this book is aimed at business owners and sales managers, any sales professional can benefit from the coaching contained herein. All of that said, we would be remiss if we didn't recommend that you get a copy of the first book and begin there. It's fairly quick read, someone calling it an "airplane ride" read.

By the way, please pay attention to the abbreviations for the four pillars below as they appear throughout the book.

Reviewing the Four Pillars of the *"Willing To Buy"* Framework

Is the prospect *"Willing To Buy"*? (WTB)

(Think of this category as the PERSONAL motivator... what's in it for anyone and everyone involved in the decision, including the key decision maker?)

Is the prospect contact the ultimate decision maker and/ or what evidence does he/she show that, as a member of the group, they themselves will make a decision and voice it to others in the decision group? This particular area deals with the personal motivation of this person to see that a decision will be made. It is in addition to the tangible business justification and speaks to what is the individual benefit for this particular person. It should also be emphasized that in order for this to be effective, the answer to this question should be from the decision maker's own words and not from the salesperson's perspective.

- Is this person (not necessarily just the decision maker) willing to make a decision, in his/her mind?
- Why is this so in the person's mind?
- What is the evidence that this is so? – verbal assurance, impending event, upper management insistence?
- Are there any other people who also must be *"Willing To Buy"* for this proposition to go forward?

Is the "Justification Evident"? (JE)

(Think of this category as the ORGANIZATIONAL motivator…what's in it for the organization?)

In other words, what is the business impact that will be used to justify the organization's commitment to any proposed solution? Has this justification been articulated by the decision maker? What are the tangible results that the prospect organization will realize?

- Is the justification evident in this contact's as well as the decision maker's mind?
- What is that justification? *(Note: Be aware that the prospect will often give you an intangible or non-qualified reason at first. It is up to the sales professional to guide the prospect as they quantify the financial impact on the business.)*

- What is the time period over which savings or value will be realized?
- Is there more than just one area in which this project will save money or add value?

Is the "Money Available"? (MA)

(Has this acquisition or commitment been BUDGETED and what is that budget?)

This topic explores the amount of money and resources (including people's time) available to effectively go ahead with any solution and implement it successfully. What evidence is there that funds and resources have been allocated to complete any project of this magnitude?

- Is there a budgeted amount for this project?
- If not, how might monies be appropriated to fund the project?
- Is the money for this project in your contact's control or must he/she go to higher management to allocate funds for this effort?
- What is the breakdown of the projected allocation of the funds (e.g. product, services, training etc.)
- What is the flexibility to go for more funds if the business case warrants it?

Is the "Decision Cycle Clear"? (DCC)

(What is the APPROVAL CYCLE and who specifically will be involved?)

This topic is needed to clarify that the decision cycle is clear, not only in the salesperson's mind, but in the decision maker's also. This is a critical element that can be used to gauge what the likelihood is that after all the survey/discovery, demo (if appropriate) and proposal work, a decision will be made.

- What is the sign-off path through management once your contact agrees with your recommendation?
- Are there hidden parties who may need to be sold separately?
- Is it appropriate for you, and what must you be prepared for, to go either with your contact or separately to the other parties to make your case?

After what seems to be all other questions have been answered, what else could keep this project from moving forward? (Have you now considered all factors in the decision making process?)

Introduction

As we write this, it's been three years since ***"Willing To Buy"©; A Questioning Framework for Effective Closing"*** © hit the bookstands (well, mostly Amazon and Barnes and Noble). My good friend and co-author Dan Schultheis and I have been overwhelmed at the positive response from the professional sales community. We were particularly proud of the blog Charles Green of *The Trusted Advisor* created touting our book. Thanks so much, Charlie!

Those of you who read the first book will recall that Dan and I would engage in what we called "jam sessions" during the writing phase. At those weekly sessions we would kick around ideas about how to get our points across and what concepts would readily resonate with our audience. Those jam sessions generated many concrete examples and even new ideas; far too many to be covered in the one book alone. So, we set aside a list of topics to be addressed in future releases or follow up works.

Both Dan and I have managed sales teams, of course, and have become somewhat opinionated about the entire sales process. The first book dealt primarily with the qualification and disqualification process. As you may recall, the entire *"Willing To Buy"* (WTB ®) Framework is based on the human aspect of selling and buying. Used properly, the Framework is what we call "product and market agnostic". We believe that it works well whether you sell software systems or real estate, cars or forklifts. Sales people engaged in selling those products are often so obsessed with discussing the relative features, functions and differentiations of their products that the buyer becomes a bit player in the entire process. That very common yet unfortunate behavior pattern is something we, as sales professionals ourselves, feel needs to change. We'll get back to discussing our view of good and bad behavior shortly.

Over the past several weeks, Dan and I have also spent a great deal of time discussing the nature of metrics as it relates to sales success. To be certain, you need to do a fair amount of prospecting to find even one closable deal. It simply goes with the territory. Authors of other books often suggest very specific ratios of "many to one". All well and good but not where the rubber meets the road. In fact, everyone and I mean everyone can force themselves to make a certain number of cold calls on a given day and enter them as "complete" in their CRM system. (By the way, we try to avoid acronyms. So, for those not familiar, CRM is Customer Relationship Management).

Yes, metrics do play a role, but if you embrace the '"*Willing To Buy*" Framework', every "touch", every interaction with the prospect is an opportunity to gather information. Where WTB differs from other systems or approaches is that those who adopt the behavior that is part of the WTB approach view the information gathered in terms of its value to the **prospect** and not the sales representative. In other words, we are placing the buyer in the role of discerning consumer or business person rather than hapless character actor. Again, more on the importance of the role of the buyer later in the book.

So Dan and I have come to the conclusion that to get the most from the '"*Willing To Buy*" Framework', one must realize that the methodology we recommend is based upon adjusting the **behavior** of the sales professional to optimize the sales/buying process to the benefit of both (or all) parties involved.

With that in mind, we have begun the process of laying out coaching techniques that can be used to boost sales and customer satisfaction. The coaching might be done by the business owner, a sales manager or simply embraced by the salesperson. The important thing is that each and every concept be addressed with a full understanding of its importance in the sales cycle.

In the first book we adopted a style we called "dialogue" and we intend to write in the same style this time. After all, it was our professional (and personal) dialogue that started this project to begin with. Moreover, many of the folks we have spoken to about "*Willing To Buy*" have encouraged us to "do it again". And hey…they buy the books.

You might want to think of this as a "*Willing To Buy*" workbook in the sense that modifying how you go about your job each day (whether you are the owner, manager or sales person) will take real work. We can set you on that course, but you need to put in the time and truly want to adopt the necessary changes. To help you get started, at the end of each chapter we will give you a little homework to do and we encourage you to take the time to complete the very brief exercises. After all, the goal is to boost sales for you and for your company.

So, let's set off yet again on a journey that will lead to greater sales success and, hopefully, more job satisfaction.

Phil Perkins

Chapter 1

Roles and Goals; The Sales Manager

"The bottom line is, when people are crystal clear about the most important priorities of the organization and team they work with and prioritize their work around those top priorities, not only are they many times more productive, they discover they have the time they need to have a whole life."

Stephen Covey

Before I turn things over to Dan to get us started, I want to reflect back just a bit to the various jobs I've had over the years as they relate to the sales profession. I also want to begin to define our target audience for this book.

I spent the first twenty years or so of my career in corporate America. I was programmer for a while, then entered management on the technology and information systems consulting services side of the business. But in my heart I always knew that I had an entrepreneurial streak. I had that itch that demands you scratch. Now of course owning your own business necessarily means being involved in the sales process, particularly in the early days. So I rapidly learned that in the first year or two I would have three roles:

- Business Owner (and goal setter)
- Sales Manager (and process builder)
- Sales Person (and business actuator)

To some degree I still fulfill those roles, although now I have some very talented people around me who have made those roles much less stressful and demanding.

All of the above said, it has become clear over the years that each of these roles, whether fulfilled by 3 people, two people or just one entrepreneur are key to a successful sales model. So, the methodology and transactional behavior of the owners of each role needs to be evaluated and infused with the right attitude and empathy for the prospect (and his or her goals and motivators both personal and organizational) so that a successful sale is also a satisfying human interaction.

Yep, I know that sounds like just a different way to define a win/win situation and perhaps that is correct. However, as Dan and I discussed in our first jam session in preparation for this book, it is our strong belief and a fundamental tenant of the '"Willing To Buy" Framework' is that whomever represents your products and services, whether you are the owner of the company, the sales manager or the sales person, you must care MOST about achieving a win for your prospect and soon to be customer.

So, I suppose the answer to the question "who is our target audience for this book" the answer is **all of the above.**

Over the next few chapters we will discuss further the roles of everyone engaged in a successful WTB sales cycle and how goals are set and met when the principals of the '"Willing To Buy" Framework' are applied to each and every touch and transaction with prospects and clients. With that, I want to turn things over to Dan who will begin with the role of the sales manager.

Let's begin our dialogue.

Thanks Phil, the entrepreneurial job is exciting but also can be wearying because of the multiple roles owners like you have to play and swap during the business day. However, since this book is geared to sales management, I'd like to expand on that role. Sales management, whether it is the day to day responsibility of the owner or one of his surrogates. Whether it's done part-time or full-time, it requires a degree of structure and consistency to create an environment where the salespeople can close business and also develop better skills and effectiveness for handling future business.

What many people don't realize about the sales management role is that it actually encompasses four functions:

- Supervision
- Training
- Coaching
- Mentoring

What usually happens in the high transaction volume world of today is that whoever is responsible for the sales management role only has time/focus for the supervisor function. As we shall discuss a little later, supervision is a very necessary but limited function for developing a professional sales team.

Before we go any further, let me define all the sales management roles:

Supervisor – This function is about measurement of pre-defined tasks, holding people accountable and taking corrective actions for not performing the tasks required. As such, it has to do with reporting certain levels of activity as well as reviewing those levels to ensure compliance.

Trainer – This function is for imparting the skills necessary for the sales people to execute the sales process and to adequately represent the company as well as the products/services provided. These skills are usually defined in a written or verbal format to the salespeople either in an on-boarding process or over the course of their early employment with the company.

Coach – This function is what the sales manager should do as he observes the salesperson executing the defined tasks. It takes into account the different styles and skill levels, as well as experience, of each of the sales people reporting to the sales manager. This means extra effort must be taken to coach individual salespeople around the skills and information conveyed during training function. Coaching is usually what is minimized or eliminated first because of the time crunch required for getting business "in the door". It is even more limited when sales management is a part time function of a senior executive or owner.

Mentor – This function is a bit more informal and takes on showing new salespeople "the ropes" of how things actually work in the company and with customers. This area is not meant to undermine any of the other functions or structure but is an acknowledgment that there is some variance from the written rules when sales people actually engage with prospects, customers or support people. This function is usually minimal because of all the other duties associated with the sales management role.

Though these functions may seem reasonable and logical, it is the rare individual who is able to prioritize his/her time to give adequate attention to each one. What typically happens is that, other than a supervisory function, the other functions are not persued or, at the very most, are not performed on a regular basis.

So, in the sales management role, we create an environment where:

- Salespeople must report a certain level of activity
- The sales manager focuses on the results of sales and/or quota…and…
- Directs the salespeople behind in their sales transaction volume to "close more business", "prospect more" or "work harder" …and…
- Doles out penalties by reducing territories or threatening to fire the salesperson if the results don't improve

This, of course, leads to a more stressful working environment. No one in a sales management role intends for the environment to be that way. But, the harsh reality is, most sales teams and sales people operate in a very combative stressful environment inside their companies, then are expected to build good customer relationships while producing greater sales volumes.

A more appropriate way to order and implement these functions is as follows:

Trainer - Start with an assessment of what skills and information each salesperson needs, both internally and externally, to adequately do their job. This can be done by testing, by observation or even by assumption. A basic training program is then put in place for everyone based on their skills and knowledge of the product and customers. Then, follow-on individualized teaching can be based on the level of skills, knowledge and retention of the training for each individual sales person.

This teaching function has highest priority, of course, when on-boarding or restructuring the sales team to better serve the goals of the company. Teaching becomes less frequent as the sales person begins to operate in their territory. However, constant assessment by the sales manager must be continued to determine any ongoing training/reinforcement required.

Supervisor: Based on the skills and knowledge needed by the salespeople, the person responsible for the sales team must determine the behaviors and activities, in both quantity and quality that a sales person must perform. This is where the "metrics" most likely to produce sales are identified and implemented. It's not unlike producing a winning football team. You can tell a football player he needs to have tackling, running, throwing and blocking skills, but the team will only produce consistent results and improve when they are given scheduled practice activities to provide an observational opportunity for the coach.

Coach - This is the most developmentally important function of a sales management role. Unless each salesperson is observed and coached individually, the quality of their activities do not dramatically improve. The skill level tends to remain the same or progress much more slowly and worse than that, sometimes regress. So once the previous two functions have been laid out there needs to be a schedule where formal coaching takes place and the frequency is set up. Of course, that applies to formal coaching sessions. Informal sessions are important also but without a formal schedule structure, skill development cannot be assured.

Mentor - The final function of the sales management role is the finishing touch to a salesperson/sales team's development. This is where the salesperson learns from the sales manager "how it really works in the field". Mentoring usually happens when the sales manager assumes the role as a sales partner with the salesperson and makes sales calls. This is an opportunity to give guidance on the best ways to handle customer complaints and internal support conflict. It's just the wise advice the person in the sales manager role can offer that will make things go smoother for the salesperson around the structure that he must operate within.

As we move into the succeeding chapters of this book, we will talk more about the steps required to put in place a sound and consistent supervisory, training, coaching and mentoring role structure.

Although setting this approach up may seem daunting at first, even small steps toward structuring these sales management roles will provide huge benefits whether you are the entrepreneurial owner doing this as part of your many functions or a sales manager running just the sales team.

Well, Dan, *daunting* is the right word for the business of implementing the sales process, at least that was the case when I tried applying all of the sales management techniques you correctly defined with my early sales teams. Depending upon how seasoned a representative was, I would tend to limit my involvement to one or two of the four areas of focus due to time constraints and geographic separation.

Like many business owners, I found myself spending most of my time creating a business plan, translating that into metrics, putting the needed sales numbers on paper, then imparting those needs to my sales people. The "whys, wherefores and what has worked before" elements of my job as sales manager were often neglected.

Crafting a business plan that clearly defines the market segment, product and service array and differentiations from competitors is critical. I have come to believe that sales managers and sales professionals have a need to understand the business plan and even the vision the owner has in his/her go to market plan. It helps them as they begin to articulate the company's position and the reasons any buyer might be ""*Willing To Buy*"".

So your definition of the four cornerstones of impactful sales management are well articulated. If only you had been my sales coach in those early days.

Action Items for Chapter 1

- **On a piece of paper list the following:**
  - Percent of your time as a sales manager and percent of your time spent direct selling;
- **Now, fill out the following table with your actual self-evaluation:**

Role	Frequency		
	Frequent	Infrequent	Rarely
Supervising			
Training			
Coaching			
Mentoring			

- **Look at your completed table from above. Note which of the 4 functions you perform rarely.**
- **What one action could you take in the next month to address each of the functions you marked 'rarely'?**

Chapter 2

Roles and Goals; The Business Owner

"I'm convinced that about half of what separates the successful entrepreneurs from the non-successful ones is pure perseverance."

Steve Jobs

Ah yes…perseverance. Certainly business owners and leaders must have a good mix of vision, drive and "stick-to-it-iveness". And perhaps Mr. Jobs was right that the last quality rises to the top. In my case, having weathered several recessions, changes in technology, shifts in expectations in the business community and turnover in key staff, had I not have persevered, our business may have gone into the metaphorical ditch.

But to persevere, in my mind, you must always have a clear view of your goals and objectives and it is your responsibility as a business owner to articulate them to your team. Of course your goals and objectives may evolve over the years as the business landscape changes, but the business owner must be prepared to adjust.

In the early days of almost any new business, the entrepreneur, out of necessity, becomes the chief sales resource. After all, he or she understands the product or service and the overall mission better than anyone. In the first few months of ACUMEN Corporation, I found myself getting up in the morning, putting on my pinstripe suit and cap toe oxfords and hitting the streets of Washington DC to meet with prospects and tell them about our company and value proposition. The experience was both exhilarating and frightening. Of course at that point there really was no company. So my job became selling the vision…the goal.

A Timely Story

Many years later and now I have a real staff. I'm not pounding the pavement anymore. I'm now relegated to number crunching and doing some part of each of the four task areas Dan defined in the first chapter. The rest of the job has been passed on to another executive.

In considering my comments above and Dan's breakdown of the key elements of sales management, I decided it was ideal timing for a heart to heart with our Vice President for Business Development (read that as "sales"). I wanted to ensure that he was fully aware of my vision as the owner and CEO of the company and how I viewed the goals for not only this year but for the next few years.

Please indulge me a little background on our VP. He is former executive of a client company to whom I had personally sold an Enterprise Resource Planning (ERP) software system. He is articulate, personable, technically adept, focused on doing what's right for our clients and (luckily) also committed to sales growth both in the near term and year over year.

So, one day my colleague and I sat down in our conference room to discuss the key elements and defining moments in the complex sales cycle associated with business management software. Now by complex I mean that there are stages along the critical path of the selling/buying process that help to determine whether the transaction is good or bad business for both my company and the prospect. Coupled with the unwavering use of the '"*Willing To Buy*" Framework' (and assuming the sales representative maintains control of the sale cycle) following the actions associated with each stage can yield a conclusion as to whether:

- The business is closable
- It can be closed in a reasonable timeframe
- Our company wants the business at all

I must admit that during the meeting I learned a great deal about how my VP reacted to our approach from the buying side and how he viewed us as a company during the sale cycle in general. It was a unique opportunity to explore the roles on both sides of the table while both of us focused on how to leverage the collective knowledge to better our company.

Dan's Observation on Business Owners

As we mentioned in the first book, Dan and I pull no punches with each other in terms of providing advice and counsel. We have explored everything from writing styles to deep seated beliefs on the ethics of business. So, I wasn't surprised when Dan provided the following observation. I don't know that these are his exact words, but you'll catch the meaning.

"You know Phil, you're like many business owners and entrepreneurs. You look for and hire people you think can do what you do. But no one can replicate your skill set, your vision and certainly not your heartfelt commitment to your business. The best you can hope for is a team of folks to provide certain skill sets that in the aggregate can fulfill your role as time goes on. Until you realize that, you won't be comfortable moving to the next phase of your career."

I have certainly come to understand that observation and take it to heart. In my case I absolutely expected others that I hired to "get" that our company is special, that our integrity is beyond reproach, that our intentions are always good, that our products are hand-picked to provide demonstrable value to our clients, and that our services are delivered by the finest professionals in the business.

So with Dan's cautionary comment in mind, I approached the meeting with my sales VP with two of the four functions of sales management Dan defined at the forefront. I wanted to provide coaching and mentoring. And I wanted the process to continue indefinitely, allowing the sales VP to handle the supervision and core training of sales resources (and providing the coaching necessary at the next level as new sales representatives are hired).

Narrowing in On My Ongoing Role

As a result of that meeting, my colleague and I decided to more fully define our roles as it relates to sales. His would be the more traditional day to day metric focused sales management function. My contribution would be in the following areas:

- Defining the market segments to be addressed
- Working with the marketing folks to create/refine the messaging (after all the original message was mine!)
- Defining and refining the go to market strategy
- Coaching and mentoring the sales VP so that he could push the messaging down to sales reps and out to our prospects

As a result of the at least temporary parsing of the responsibilities associated with the sales management function, I was getting some measure of the skill set and focus I had looked for to begin with. Also, I am convinced that the more frequently my colleague and I have these sessions the more comfortable I will become. I do want to be clear that I have always tried to be open to new ideas and certainly our sales Vice President has some great new approaches to share and implement. All companies must move forward and not be afraid to evolve.

Well, Dan, I'm being a bit reflective here, but you drew my attention to the unique and singular role of the entrepreneur or business owner. I want to pass to you for your comments on the roles and parameters that business owners can adopt to further the goals of their business and boost sales.

Over to you.

Wow Phil, thanks for opening up your thought process on this whole entrepreneurial idea.

I believe there is a certain type of intelligence needed to start, run and grow a successful business venture. As you know, there are many types of intelligence; mathematical, artistic, spatial, etc.

I would like to suggest adding a new one called quote "entrepreneurial intelligence". This is the inborn ability to handle multiple roles at one time and fluidly switch from one to another as needed. I guess it's a sort of "on demand" role execution. However, even with this outstanding ability, there is a potential drawback when one starts to build a business.

A psychologist friend of mine once told me there are different types of abilities when it comes to teaching skills to others.

- First, there's a group who doesn't know all the things they know and therefore can't teach others
- Second, there's a group who know what they know but can't articulate it in a way people will learn
- Third, there's a group who know what they know and can convey this but don't have the skills or patience to ensure it's grounded in the business "DNA" of their employees

With the weight of building a company resting squarely on the shoulders of the founder and owner, there usually is precious little time for teaching and coaching others.

Therefore, I would suggest that when an entrepreneur takes on the role of sales manager, he/she will naturally embrace the mentoring part of the role. However, the other three roles are not in the owner's comfort zone.

Before you brilliant entrepreneurs there take offense at my points, I will tell you it is not the role of the entrepreneur to understand/use all of the sales manager functions. But, in reality just make sure these functions are at least acknowledged as being minimally utilized until the company has grown large enough to dedicate a management resource, either part or full time to this sales management role.

Our most important role, by Phil's own admission, is making sure that the vision held by everyone in the company is a mirror image of the one in the owner's mind.

By default, this is a weighty responsibility and as such doesn't allow much time for supervision, training and coaching. One big challenge for the entrepreneurial owner is that they must integrate all of the demands across all of the roles they play. This is such a part of who they are and what's expected of them that most feel that anyone could do what they do if only these others were as dedicated and hard working as the entrepreneur.

It's hard to accept but, fact is, others need more specific definitions to their roles, skills to perform those roles, and supervision and coaching to make sure those skills are embedded in their day-to-day work.

The question may come, reading my position on this topic, "OK, my company seems to be doing okay without all this formal role definition, why fix what isn't broken?". My answer: It's not about doing okay today but about how to prosper when your company is 3X or 4X the size.

Just like a professional level sports team, a sales team needs a "system", both to learn and be coached on to be better. It's been said that on average people are average. Many entrepreneurs feel they can build a superior sales team by searching for a "LeBron James" or "Tom Brady" type salesperson. This only leads to frustration because there aren't that many "naturally" occurring in any market. So, long term it leads the entrepreneur to be frustrated when they can't seem to find many, if any, of them. Unfortunately, until the owner realizes he/she must build his sales team through selection, training and coaching, he/she will have a "revolving door" of sales people coming in and out of this business. The truth is there aren't that many "natural" LeBron or Brady salespeople. What exists are many, many average or above people who with an effective coaching "system" can be molded into a top performing professional sales team. It isn't magic but coaching does take time, consistency and patience.

As Phil said at the beginning of this chapter, it's all about "stick-to-it-iveness", not only when it comes to vision and goals but also structure and role definition. Thank you again, Phil, for your "peek behind the curtain" and your candor in addressing this not only sensitive but pervasive entrepreneurial mindset.

Dan Schultheis and Phil Perkins

Action Items for Chapter 2

- As the owner/sales executive/sales manager, in your judgment, which 3 or 4 skills/talents does a salesperson in your company need to be successful:

    1. _____

    2. _____

    3. _____

    4. _____

- Now, fill out the following table by listing your salespeople and how they rate on a scale (from 1- outstanding to 5 – poor).

Salesperson Name	Skills (Rating)			
_____	1. _____	2. _____	3. _____	4.
_____	1. _____	2. _____	3. _____	4.
_____	1. _____	2. _____	3. _____	4.
_____	1. _____	2. _____	3. _____	4.
_____	1. _____	2. _____	3. _____	4.

- Finally, observe your skills analysis of your sales team and choose one area for each individual for you to focus on with them to improve their performance.

Chapter 3

Roles and Goals; The Sales Representative

"To me, job titles don't matter. Everyone is in sales. It's the only way we stay in business."

Harvey McKay

"Feet on the street"

"Face in the place"

"Carrying a bag"

"Smile and dial"

I've heard those phrases associated with the job of the sales representative for more years than I care to admit. All portray the position as one of nearly robotic repetition in my mind. Call the client, hopefully get the appointment, trudge over for a face to face meeting and hope you make a good enough impression to offer up your solution.

I'm going to continue to reveal some realities associated with being a business owner. For instance, I have certainly been guilty of repetitive hiring errors looking for the James or Brady stars that Dan mentions. I have been distracted by engaging personalities, the gift of gab (that trap is almost a sin these days) and declarations of past success in related businesses.

I have pursued various methods in trying to find the ideal fit for our complex sale cycle and process. For instance, wouldn't it seem logical that a sales representative hired from a company that represents the type of business to whom you offer your products and services would be an ideal candidate? After all, the representative can speak the language, talk the talk and walk the walk. That may indeed be a realistic mode of hiring but this method has had mixed results in our company.

Since ours is a consultative business, I have also tried utilizing gregarious and well liked consultants in the sales role. Some did very well for a while but invariably fell back into the analytical processes that made them solid consultants to begin with. Often that resulted in "analysis paralysis" (sorry for the over used terminology but it fits in this case) and failure to launch in the sales sense.

So regardless of what your product or service is you really have to determine what type of individual will likely succeed in fulfilling the mission of the business via the process of selling. What factors must be considered:

- Market knowledge (target markets)?
- Successful track record?
- Gift of gab?
- Geographical familiarity?
- Analytical skills?
- Empathy?
- Listening skills?
- Ability to articulate ideas and concepts?
- Written word skills?
- Being presentable?

Yep! All of the above.

But let's face it, finding all of those attributes in one person is very difficult if not impossible. And if you set the standard that high, whether you are the business owner or the sales manager, you are bound to be disappointed and even disillusioned.

So, let's take a look at a more realistic view of the both the sales representative's role and how a manager might go about optimizing those important attributes that any hard working sales rep might bring to the job.

In chapter one I refer to the sales representative as the "business actuator". Let's first have a look at the word actuate so that my meaning will become clear.

Actuate

To cause (a machine or device) to operate.

"the pendulum actuates an electrical switch"

To cause (someone) to act in a particular way; motivate.

"the defendants were actuated by malice"

While it may not seem obvious, I think both uses of the word are in play in this case. If you accept "machine" as a metaphor for your company, the business actuator is one who causes that particular machine to operate. I think you would agree that many companies are carried on the backs of the outstanding sales person or persons who drive revenue and profit. So yes, I think that definition fits.

Of course, the second definition is a more traditional view of the sales representative's role. After all, we want our reps to "motivate" the buyer to "act in a particular way" by buying our product or service.

My point here is that we must give due respect to the importance of the position and provide the environment were Dan's "average" sales resource can approach LeBron James or Tom Brady results.

Zeroing In On Key Attributes

Take a look back at my list of highly desirable attributes above. Let's all agree that finding all of those in one sales candidate is unlikely (although highly desirable). If you were somehow restricted to two of the attributes, what two would you choose? (Okay, let's throw out "presentable" since no one is likely to hire a slob to represent his or her company).

I have come to the conclusion that the ability to be an effective listener coupled with the ability to articulate ideas and concepts top the list. If you read the first *"Willing To Buy"* book you know that we defined a "questioning framework". In other words, a process by which the sales professional could ask certain types of questions designed to ferret out the sales motivators (or perhaps buying motivators), both personal and organizational, associated with a given prospect. Of course, framing the questions properly is only part of the equation.

Do you remember the last time you tried to explain to a sales person what you were looking for in a car, a boat, your next home or any consumer good only to have that person begin to enumerate the many benefits of a product clearly not on your wish list? Do you remember how that felt? Of course, it can be maddening. So, I feel strongly that the most successful sales professionals are expert at actually hearing what you are saying and probing a bit further to determine how best to serve your needs.

Once the sales person has asked questions to gain clarity, you will notice that the best of the best restate what they have learned from the prospect so that mistakes in interpretation can be avoided. In this way the seller is almost crossing over to the buyer side of the table. He or she is illustrating that the requirements set forth by the buyer actually matter.

Yes, I know, that all sounds fundamental. But remember, I asked you to choose only two attributes. I'm betting that in your mind's eye you didn't immediately envision a chatty local guy, or a market specialist with a great wardrobe. But then again, maybe you did. I'll stick with my two choices. That said, you know about my poor track record.

The Value Proposition

One area where the business owner, sales manager and sales representative simply must agree upon is the full understanding of the company's "value proposition". To insure that we are on the same page I looked up the classic definition.

Value Proposition – *noun* (in marketing) an innovation, service, or feature intended to make a company or product attractive to customers.

While the initial responsibility for defining the value proposition generally falls to the business owner, the packaging of that critical business message may be the responsibility of the marketing manager, the sales manager or even occasionally (typically in smaller companies) the sales representative. The business owner is usually the one who determines:

- What we sell
- To whom we wish to sell our goods and/or services
- How we will find our buyers
- What differentiates us, our products and/or services from our competitors

Once those determinations are made, it falls to the business actuators to routinely articulate the advantages of dealing with his or her company and the value of the products and/or services. Delivering this message must be done in a consistent manner using language the buyer can understand.

In my mind, the value proposition is something that every employee should be aware of and able to discuss. It is beyond the elevator pitch in that it often goes to the core values of the company itself. You can tell when a value proposition is based in deeply seated beliefs in the company's ability to deliver the goods. It shows in how the message is delivered by everyone from the receptionist to the plant manager to the human resources manager to (and most importantly) the sales representative.

The value proposition cannot be learned simply by reading it from a company manual. In my opinion it is transmitted via mentoring on a consistent basis and ultimately adopted by employees as they see that their company backs up its claims and promises.

And of course as the business actuator, the sales representative's role is critical in getting the message out. Given the consistent training and mentoring, even the average to just above average representatives can become true believers. They can learn to use their listening skills and ability to restate the needs of the buyer to marry the opportunity to the value of the goods and services offered.

Of course, as you sales professionals who follow the '"Willing To Buy" Framework' know all too well, the sales professional is duty bound to identify those situations where our products and services are NOT the answer and expertly disengage.

Dan, as I pass this back to you, I'm sure you can see that I am a bit opinionated regarding key attributes. I'm sure you also know that I have come to believe that the role of the sales representative has been undervalued and often maligned. However, because each and every representative who truly wants to succeed as a business actuator deserves that chance, I agree with you wholeheartedly. Ultimately "good" reps can be trained and counseled so that they can deliver "great" results. Okay coach, you're up.

Thanks Phil. Nobody could ever accuse us of lacking the strength of our convictions!

I'm going to take this discussion in another direction if I may. I don't disagree with your choices of top attributes, but I'd like to shine a light on understanding and addressing the two areas that will, in fact, either inhibit or enhance those talents based on how they are used:

1. Ability to Execute

This concept is about the typical management assumption that the ability to execute the sales role comes easily to someone with a group of sales attributes/talents. I believe there is a fallacy in that assumption. To illustrate, let's look at a sporting example:

Assume we are a college golf coach looking for a talented athlete to join our golf team in college. We might start by listing the attributes/talents as you did:

- Competitive spirit
- Eye hand coordination
- Good observational skills
- Ability to focus

Let's then say we found two or three candidates that exhibited some or all of these strengths. We would then choose the best one based on observations and discussions, then just basic gut feel.

Suppose we told this new recruit that, "we want to be the best golf team with the best competition record and to finish at the top of our division".

Once we saw the appropriate head nodding from him/her, would we say, "now that you know our team goals and ultimate end result, I expect you to practice a lot and get better so you can help us".

I know I'm getting a little silly here but I'm doing this to make a point. Even though I agree with your belief in the importance of business actuator metaphor, it is what we do with the raw talent that makes the difference and not just the presence of that talent.

To use another analogy, I know an army needs talented/focused/determined soldiers to be able to win battles but, without rigorous, repetitive training and reinforcement, those talented people will wind up as causalities instead of victors.

Now, I may not be going down a path here that will make me a lot of friends in the owner/executive ranks. However, the reality, from my experience and repeating a point I made earlier in the book, entrepreneurs think anybody can do what they have done and how they have sold if they only worked harder. This internal entrepreneurial DNA many times blinds those leaders to the fact that you CANNOT allow your salespeople immediate autonomy in how they execute in their territories. Just like we couldn't allow our new golf student to play the game his way without giving him drills, exercises and challenges, then observing/evaluating and coaching him to improve.

The role of the salesperson is essential since we will not win anything without our "soldiers". However, we must always realize that developing a strong and consistent sales role is a twofold process:

1. Find the candidates with the best combination of desired attributes/ talents and
2. Do NOT assume they know how to use them in pursuit of the goals we give them.

2. Matching Personal & Corporate Desires

Here I go again jumping into the fire!

When owners talk about company goals, vision and results with their salespeople, they look for reactions like nodding in agreement or enthusiastic "high fiving" to indicate they are in synch with the owner and are "all in".

But, let me burst that bubble a little. In reality, salespeople (just like all of us) are no different from their prospects when it comes to their personal *"Willing To Buy"* pillar. They are also listening to that FM station; WIIFM (What's In It For Me?").

I'm not suggesting that salespeople are not somewhat interested in what the "business" succeeds at, but the volume of WIIFM drowns out company interest with personal interest. Now, what's frustrating for most owners/ executives is that you can get your employees to put their hand over their hearts and pledge allegiance to the company, but you can't drown out their personal FM station. There is no way to <u>force</u> that allegiance.

Why do I bring this up? It's not that this reality will go away. We all have it. We acknowledge that it's there in all of our people, including salespeople and we, as leaders, must put safeguards in place to ensure that there is an actual and understood "link" between each salesperson's FM station and the company's. This is usually somewhat different for each salesperson and therein lies the difficulty managing this.

Phil, though I'll cycle back and agree with your point about finding the "best of the pack" based on our success attributes. This is only the starting gate for strengthening this important "business actuator" role.

When I said earlier in the book that, "on average people are average", I wasn't being critical. I was merely suggesting that, though we should diligently hunt for talent for this role, we should count more on developing the frontline troops to be effective than on finding that "diamond in the rough" who will carry the team.

Dan, your points are well taken. So at this point we agree that being discerning in the hiring process and making a commitment to giving those that we do hire the proper supervision, coaching, training and mentoring will help to foster good results. In the following chapters, we will take an in depth look at how we approach each of those management and leadership responsibilities.

Action Items for Chapter 3

* What are the Top 3 skills needed across your sales team:

      1. _____

      2. _____

      3. _____

* In your training/coaching role, can you personally train and coach these skills? (Y /N)

      * If yes, which practice activities would you have them practice for you?

      _____

      _____

      _____

      _____

      * If no, as a "head coach", you must identify an "assistant coach" to train and coach the above skills.

Chapter 4

Vision to Actuation; Driving It Home

*"Building a visionary company requires one percent vision
and 99 percent alignment"*

Jim Collins and Jerry Porras in "Built to Last"

As chapter three was completed, Dan and I met for what would become
one of the most spirited jam sessions we've had since the early days of our
first book together. In the last chapter I spent a great deal of time on the
hiring process while Dan properly pointed out the importance of imposing
"rigor" on members of the sales team. It is quite humbling to realize
that I too have fallen into the trap of hiring based upon an incomplete
understanding of the sales representative's "out of the box" ability to drive
sales and to be that business actuator that I needed.

In terms of how the business owner approaches filling key positions, I have
now come to accept that most of us would dearly love to clone ourselves so
that our employees share our vision. It would be nice if they just naturally
fell into line and did what it takes every day to help meet company goals
and objectives. We want team members who believe in not only our
products and services, but who strongly support and articulate the positive
attributes that differentiate us from our competition.

Regardless of what business you are in, your company has a certain
dynamic. It is more than just corporate culture. It is about the way your
clients and employees feel about the company and its direction. To control
that dynamic and properly set expectations for prospects, clients and
employees, it is important that systematic approach be applied to giving
the sales representatives and others in the organization not only the usual
tools but also the daily (and situationally appropriate) attention they need
to succeed.

The Sales Process as a Project

Since Dan and I both come from technology backgrounds, it became obvious early on that you might apply project management and tracking methodology to the sales process. In my case, our company ACUMEN Corporation was founded and became successful as a result of our belief that there are certain techniques that can be employed to insure consistent and measurable positive results in the implementation of complex software systems. To be certain, managing a project depends less on a pretty Gantt chart and a lot more on setting realistic goals and finding a way to measure success along the way. Success along the critical path also depends upon the skillset that allows certain trained/learned behaviors to pave the way.

All well run projects have several attributes in common. Here are just a few:

- **Project Narrative -** The pre-project discovery process should yield a narrative of what areas of concern need to be addressed by the software, tool or process being implemented. The narrative should include a clear definition of the goals to be attained and by what means success along the critical path will be determined and measured. At ACUMEN Corporation we call this the discovery document.
- **Assumption Set -** In software implementation projects, an assumption might be "it is assumed that all key stakeholders will attend the training sessions in their respective areas of interest". In a sales process, an assumption might be something like "it is assumed that the prospect has a budget allocated and will inform us of said budget". Those of you already familiar with the '"*Willing To Buy*" Framework' will recognize this part of the process as the "Money Available (MA)" pillar.
- **Illustration of Dependencies –** During a software project, the dependency might be availability of a third party consultant at an exact time on the critical path. In a complex sales process, availability of a corresponding consulting or technical resource to add credibility to the value proposition is a solid example of a dependency.

- **Time Pegged Project Plan –** I am a believer in the building of a graphic representation of the who, what and when of any type of project. Many modern CRM (Customer Relationship Management) packages allow a sales representative to build a plan defining a step by step process leading to closure. Moreover, these plans can be made visible to sales management and business owners. In the world of '*"Willing To Buy"'*, one might time peg the gaining of information to clarify the needed data in the four pillars of the framework rather than simply the milestones such as first call, presentation, demo, proposal as is often the fallback. You will find a review of the four pillars of the framework in the Preface.

- **Weekly Project Accountability Report –** In the world of software implementation (you'll pardon my frequent references to the software marketplace, my baseline for perspective) a weekly report to both the client and management is invaluable in measuring the progress of the project and setting the stage for corrective action if and where necessary. In sales, the representatives should be given a standard report format and required to submit it for top prospects.

What has become obvious, particularly over the past few years, is that companies with a track record of success in growing through sales define a critical path during the sale cycle. That process is very much as a software company, heavy equipment manufacturer or construction firm would utilize during a software implementation, deployment of new capital equipment or completion of a business process consulting engagement. In other words, there are steps to be followed in the typical sale cycle which at a minimum may include:

- Demand generation (finding the "suspects", or those likely to have a need)
- Initial qualification
- Deeper discovery and qualification (hopefully using the '*"Willing To Buy"*Framework'). This is likely the first opportunity to establish the assumption set and dependencies since deep qualification tends to root out the red flags and deeper opportunities, along with decision makers and criteria for deciding

- Preparation of the Value Proposition
- Demonstration of the product (whether it be software as mentioned above or a new forklift)
- …and finally asking for the business

You may note that determining the assumption set and dependencies as early in the process as possible allows the sales manager to utilize an "if then else" decision process. That classic approach allows he or she to provide the right level of monitoring and coaching to insure the sales process is headed in the right direction. Moreover, quick recognition of the deviations in the starting assumptions and success or failure of the dependencies can allow for adjustments to the course of action on the critical path.

The point here is that defining a set of rules by which the sales team can operate makes the sales process more measurable, such that the sales manager can make corrections along the way using additional training and coaching. In the next few chapters we'll discuss when supervision is needed and when coaching, teaching and mentoring is the correct course of action. However, the starting point is a clearly defined plan for success based upon the stated goals of the owners of the company, whether that be by increase in revenue by product line, expansion of product selection, or incremental sales to existing clients.

Alignment:

At the beginning of every chapter we offer up a quote that helps illustrate or illuminate the points to come. In preparing for this chapter we had many, many to choose from that fit the bill. But what better source than "Built to Last"? We particularly liked the reference to "alignment" since Dan and I had discussed that concept in detail during our last session.

In this case, alignment means insuring that employees understand and can execute on the vision and goals of the ownership. No matter how charismatic the owner(s) may be, it is clear that the 'whys' and 'wherefores' of the company direction, mores and processes need to be reinforced with every employee in the company as frequently as necessary to insure consistent execution. We'll dig deeper into the importance of alignment in the next chapter.

With that understanding in mind, I'm going to pass to Dan to further discuss goals, execution and rigor in the sales department.

Thanks, Phil. I appreciate your description of the project management attributes you've used successfully in your company. I agree with you that these attributes are similar to those needed in any "sales project".

I'd like to show this by paralleling your attributes only with a "sales project" flavor:

Project Narrative:

The sales project narrative is the early dialogue between the prospective customer and the salesperson that defines the scope of the problem to be solved and the impact of having solved it for the prospect's company. This is not necessarily a short discussion depending on the factors involved in the solution and may take several meetings/discussions. It also has to do with the financial, time and personal impact associated with **NOT** solving the problem, including the obstacles in the way and the previous attempts to solve them.

Assumption Set:

The sales assumption set is based on the money, resources and time the prospect is willing to commit to solve this problem. Just as in a standard project, it is a mistake to allow the project sponsor (aka prospect) not to be involved in the "project" to implement the sales solution to their stated problem. This sales assumption set is critical to get in place if an order is to be expected, let alone implemented.

Illustration of Dependencies:

The majority of dependencies in the sales project are associated with the people involved in the decision to be made. They are both those who are directly involved in the decision making process as well as those influencers who are indirectly involved. Once all parties are identified, then a '"*Willing To Buy*" Framework' can be developed for each person, thus ensuring a comprehensive view of not only who is involved in the initial decision, but also what role they might play in the implementation of the solution. At times there may just one person involved but more often than not there will be more.

Time Pegged Project Plan:

Of course in sales, timing is critical both in when the decision will be made and why. What is key to determine is not only when the decision will be made but when the positive impact of that decision will be felt by the prospect. This is the true "sales project" completion date of the scope.

Once the time pegging is determined, whether the sales project will happen can then be assessed from the prospect's urgency.

If the prospect would:

- **Like** to have the solution implemented – This is lowest level of urgency. The project will not likely happen in any predictable timeframe
- **Need** to have it – This shows a bit more urgency but can only be validated by identifying how long the prospect has "needed" the problem solved. The longer the time, the less likely now is the time
- **Want** to have it - This adds an emotional component to the above need and therefore adds a little more fuel to the fire of solving the problem
- **Must** have it – This is where the prospect gives some impending event that makes the solution an absolute necessity to avoid the negative impact from that impending event

So, as you can see, the 'Time Pegging' is the attribute of our sales project that gives our "project" a greater degree of predictability; either that it will happen or it won't.

Weekly Project Accountability Report:

As Phil indicated earlier in this chapter, once a project has its scope, timeframe and sponsor(s) defined, there must be regular meetings held by the project manager to assess status, any specific to do's and the likelihood of achieving the desired completion date. So too is it with sales. The weekly meetings are essential to keep the sales team, including management, informed as to where to place added focus, where to adjust expectations (both of the sales team as well as the prospects) and when to abandon the prospect opportunity altogether because of the probability of a bad outcome (not getting the sale).

As Phil mentioned, many people think Sales Force Automation (SFA) is what's needed to produce better results. While SFA is certainly an important component of a consistent high performing sales team, the addition of the project management approach coupled with the '"*Willing To Buy*" (WTB) Framework' will provide the needed "Why behind the What". For using SFA only will define sales milestones (quantity) but will likely miss the WTB structured management approach (quality) that completes the structure that produces high performing salespeople and teams.

By understanding and paralleling the successful project management/ WTB approach in sales, we enable the most elusive attribute a sales manager needs to have: predictability. When this approach is applied to sales and combined with an expected level of sales activity, both in quantity and quality, the owner/sales executive can feel confident that consistent, exceptional results will occur.

Action Items for Chapter 4

- List all the unique steps that could occur during a normal sales cycle;
- Now, sequence these steps as you've seen them occurring during the sales cycle.
- Take a sample list of your current opportunities and place them where they are on each step Keep this list for the Chapter 7 exercise

Chapter 5

On The Same Page; Alignment and Engagement

"There are only three measurements that tell you nearly everything you need to know about your organization's overall performance: employee engagement, customer satisfaction, and cash flow. It goes without saying that no company, small or large, can win over the long run without energized employees who believe in the mission and understand how to achieve it."

Jack Welch, former CEO of GE

I was driving to work today thinking about how I might begin this chapter when I was given a little gift. As I often do this time of year, I was tuned into the NFL channel on Sirius radio. As a pretty average American guy during the fall and winter months, I can't seem to get enough football. Perhaps it's the pure escapism of it. Who knows?

In any case, the commentators were talking about the traits of the teams with the best records in the NFL as opposed to those of the teams that had become "cellar dwellers". Invariably, one of the speakers said, it was matter of to what degree the players "bought in" to the vision and methodologies put forth by the head coach and his staff. BFO! (Sorry, I had always promised our readers we wouldn't use acronyms...that's "blinding flash of the obvious". At least it wasn't one of my technical terms!)

As it is on a football team so it is with companies. Certainly coaches can draw out the x's and o's on a whiteboard to map out plays and tell the team to "bring your A game", but the really successful franchises define a mission and a methodology to achieve the mission. The best coaches illustrate how each man plays a role in carrying out the mission and how each job is key to winning as a team.

During the conversation, I was intrigued as the sportscasters called out certain players who seemed to be "doing their jobs" but not necessarily playing a greater role in actuating the overall mission. They chalked that behavior up to failure of the coaching staff to fully articulate and justify the mission. Sure, you might think that the mission of every team is to win the Super Bowl, but the most successful coaches will tell you that that goal can only be accomplished with a set of steps that are predefined, explained and executed across the enterprise. Sounds like a very sound process but consider the fact that during any given season only a handful of teams have winning records and only two make the Super Bowl. So as important as the alignment of goals and steps to achieve them are to the proper execution of a football game, very few organizations can point to years of success based upon that even handed, step by step methodology and team buy-in that got them there.

Back to Business

Fully acknowledging that the NFL is a business and a very successful one, let's turn our attention back to our own organizations. Last chapter we spent a bit of time acknowledging the importance of alignment within every business. As I mentioned, Dan and I recently discussed how the concepts and processes that comprise the '"*Willing To Buy*" Framework' seem quite straight forward upon first reading, but need constant watering and weeding to yield great results.

In other words, to boost sales to the degree required by growing organizations, a commitment must be made by owners and managers to link the concepts in WTB to the overall mission of the company. Sales people who think of themselves as professionals have a real need to know that every minute of each work day will yield results. After all, the true professionals already have a virtual compulsion to ask "why" and "how". And management has a responsibility to answer those questions.

As we were researching the importance of alignment in every company, it became obvious that there were actually two components to gaining buy-in for '"*Willing To Buy*"' or any major corporate goal, *corporate alignment* and *employee engagement.* I'm a firm believer in defining terms in a timely fashion as our dialogue continues. Below are definitions of these terms as provided by BusinessDictionary.com:

Corporate Alignment:

"The linking of organizational goals with the employees' personal goals. Requires common understanding of purposes and goals of the organization, and consistency between every objective and plan right down to the incentive offers."

Employee Engagement:

"Emotional connection an employee feels toward his or her employment organization, which tends to influence his or her behaviors and level of effort in work related activities."

I find it quite interesting that the word 'emotional' is used in the second definition. Growing up in corporate America, I was always taught to keep your emotions in check. But this definition is spot on when you consider why people actually excel at their jobs. Sure, you often run into people who say things like "I love my job" or on occasion "I hate my job". But I find (and I think Dan would agree) that an emotional connection is actually demonstrated by the relish you bring to doing your job and your willingness to go a step or two beyond your job description to help actuate the corporate mission. And that level of commitment can usually only be attained when you:

- Understand and even (hopefully) agree with the goals the company has established
- Understand and agree with the methodology by which the goals may be attained
- Understand and accept how your role in the company helps to make the methodology work

In an article on Bloomberg Business Online written by the staff of the Corporate Executive Board (CEB) to facilitate the three points above a company must be willing to:

1. **Measure the specific behaviors required to achieve organizational goals.**

   (WTB Note: These behaviors are easily identified inside the *"Willing To Buy"* Framework'. The questioning, listening, rewording, questioning, listening rigor is well defined as it relates to sales excellence)

2. **Focus Action-Planning on daily activities.**

   (WTB Note: In the Framework, as with most sales disciplines, daily activities are well defined. In many cases, however, these activities are quite different than most sales "systems" and require a customer focus that takes time and practice to fully implement.)

3. **Involve line management.**

   (WTB Note: As it relates to the *"Willing To Buy"* Framework', this CEB recommendation suggests involving not only owners in pushing the mission and methodology down the organization but also sales managers and leaders as well.)

So moving from mission to specific goals, to corporate alignment to employee engagement requires a level of routine communication and follow-up that some in management (and some in sales themselves) may not be used to delivering. Dan and I would suggest that these naysayers aren't positioned to sustain and grow the organization for the long term. Those willing to take the time stand to create what author and corporate CEO Walt Zeglinski calls a "committed culture". Here's how he describes this unique and productive entity:

"Engaged with a clear understanding of its goals, a Committed Culture both maximizes the potential of its employees and consistently achieve goals. It's the healthiest of work environments – what every organization should strive to achieve. Employees work with clarity and purpose and, although they might not always meet all goals, they stay committed to an action plan to fulfill them. Because they have an understanding of what success looks and feels like, they can develop the attitudes and beliefs that release achievement drive. This provides the energy and motivation to execute with accountability.

A Committed Culture isn't foolproof. An aligned, engaged culture must be nurtured to sustain performance standards. Regular progress reviews can ensure employees are meeting their goals and whether corrective action is necessary to stay on track.

Why strive for a Committed Culture? When your work force is fully engaged and clear about its goals, your employees will be loyal to the core. And a loyal work force is one that naturally inspires loyal customers – emotionally satisfied customers who refer new customers to you and generate repeat sales. An organization that develops a Committed Culture has unlocked the secret to successful plan execution and profitable growth. It has created a culture of positive accountability."

Committing to *"Willing To Buy"*

I'm going to turn this discussion over to Dan to further explore how the '*"Willing To Buy"* Framework' can help to create a committed culture inside your sales organization at least and your entire enterprise at most. As a CEO myself, I have seen how this logical yet rigorous process can foster alignment with company goals and energize and engage the sales team and those who support them.

Over to you, Dan.

Thanks, Phil. Your discussion about alignment has caused me to reflect on the multiple organizations I have helped over the years clarify what they are about and how to break it down in an understandable form for their employees.

There unfortunately has existed a belief, with many in senior management that, "If I paint a vision of the future in my communications to the employees, it will be intuitively obvious to all that hear the words what they should do to ensure that they are doing their part to make sure the "vision" becomes the "reality".

The real story is that most employees begin their employment with a company because they need a job. Even though there may be a lot of "high fives" when one begins their career in an organization, that exuberance melts away if the senior executives haven't done the hard work of developing an "alignment path" for employees to follow.

Let me expand on the alignment path idea. Assume a vision that is stated by the CEO to be three times the current size and to have increased market share from 10% to 30% in five years.

Everyone hears the vision and is excited about the future, but, as Steve Danish, a goals achievement expert said to me, "Almost all of us can say what our 5 year goal is but very few of us can say what specifically we're going to do tomorrow to move toward that goal".

Therein lies the challenge with insuring alignment between vision and specific activities. This challenge must be met with a type of "reverse engineering" process that moves from vision goals (which are actual results) back to the categories/segments that must be focused on to achieve the goals. From here, the types of activities (both marketing and selling) must be identified and applied in the direction of the categories/segments identified in the previous step. And, finally, a set of behaviors must be determined, measured and managed to ensure that the proper skills are developed in the employees to accomplish the overall objectives.

Let's take this conceptual discussion and apply it to a real world situation. I suggest we use the NFL team that Phil mentioned earlier, to illustrate an alignment effort.

Articulated Vision for the Team (usually by the GM): Example: To win the division title two years in a row.

Categories/Segments to focus on (usually by the Head Coach; sometimes called the team strategy): Example: Develop a strong and dependable running game and tough passing defense.

Activities essential to support achievement of the categories/segments (usually by the assistant coaches): Example: (we will assume for this example that the best trade and draft choices have been made to support the vision) Identify the specific activities as well as their quantity and frequency during practices e.g. run 20 scrimmage running plays per practice alternating running backs, run another 20 scrimmage passing plays per practice where the safeties are alternated.

Observe and Coach the players on improving the activities identified in the previous step: Example: Suggesting a different running pattern to a back who doesn't run laterally or how to keep the receiver in front of the safety on a long passing play.

As you can see from this short example, alignment takes a significant amount of thought and "reverse engineering" to have the best chance of achieving the desired vision results from the GM.

This same process is what is needed to ensure alignment and to have the best chance for player engagement.

If we apply this to a business model, it might look something like this:

Articulated Vision for the Organization (usually by the CEO/Owner):
Example: To be 3X larger in 5 years and grow market penetration from 10% to 30%.

Categories/Segments to focus on (usually by the COO/Marketing Executive; sometimes called the marketing strategy): Example: Develop a strong presence in the healthcare and manufacturing industry segments)

Activities essential to support achievement of the categories/segments (usually by the Sales Executive): Example: Identify the specific activities as well as their quantity and frequency during practices, e.g. attend conferences in the healthcare and manufacturing industries to develop a target prospect list, develop marketing plans for the Top 10 Prospect companies in each segment, and target executives to contact in each of these companies with target timeframes.

Observe and Coach the players on improving the activities identified in the previous step (usually by the Sales Manager(s) - This includes both a quantity and quality management effort:

- **Quantity:**
  - Have meeting with one executive in each of the identified prospect companies in the first quarter of the year
  - Propose a solution to at least 3 of these prospect companies in the first half of the year

- **Quality:**
  - Coach the salesperson before and after each of the above activities on improving their effectiveness in execution

This is the area where the WTB framework can help with the "how to" of the activities identified in the quantity step. Though the WTB framework always improves the closing effectiveness, without identified activities and their quantities, the WTB pillars will not be as effective as they could be. This is not unlike trying to help a running back with his running style/

techniques without defining the plays & frequency to provide examples for the coach to advise against.

One final note: this is an iterative process. It won't ever be final and never be changed. Just like a professional sports team, practice and a coaching framework is the best chance for not only achieving the vision, but for building in learning and repeatability to the process. [1]

---

[1] Walt Zeglinski is CEO and Managing Partner for Performax ROI, a growth acceleration firm that helps clients to create value-centric cultures that exceed customer and investor expectations. Walt has over 25 years of successful experience maximizing talent with his practical solutions for complex business challenges. He has worked with executive teams across most industries and around the world. For more information, visit http://www.performax-roi.com.

Action Items for Chapter 5

* Does your company have a specific revenue objective for the current year?

     Yes _____   No _____

* If yes, is this goal broken down by segments (e.g. geography, size, industry, product, etc.)

     Yes _____   No _____

* Are there identified activities/behaviors/tactics specifically for each segment?

     Yes _____   No _____

If 2 out of 3 of the above questions are No, go back to question 1 and get started to change it, if possible.

Chapter 6

By the Numbers; Goal Setting to Actuation

"Most 'impossible' goals can be met simply by breaking them down into bite size chunks, writing them down, believing them, and then going full speed ahead as if they were routine."

Don Lancaster

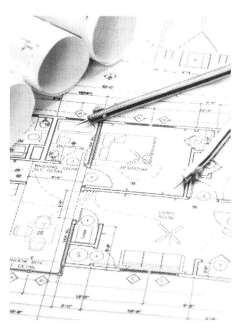

As we get into the "hard stuff", the down and dirty work it takes to actuate a corporate vision, we will change the sequence of our roles and goals exercise and begin by looking at the additional responsibilities of business owners in todays' economy. After all, everything in business is top down...or should be. Once we step through this process, we will be able to see how the *'"Willing To Buy"'* process can help in insuring the model for success is understood and executed by the sales team day in and day out.

Let's get started.

If you are a business owner you have to ask yourself..."how well do I know my own business?". Certainly in the early days of most businesses, the founders spend a good deal of time deciding what products and or services to sell and to whom. That sort of strategic planning takes a good deal of time and study. But once the offering and market or markets are identified, you're off and running. The owner and whomever is involved with the company early on are taught to engage with the appropriate buyers and offer up the unique and focused "value proposition" with pride and enthusiasm.

Of course sometimes that works and sometimes it doesn't. According to Gallop, 50% of US businesses fail in their first five years. To me that's a staggering number and quite frightening. I'm certainly happy we're in our 27th year. But I am convinced that the businesses that do survive (if not necessarily flourish) have a very good collective understanding of who they are, who their customers are, what their customers expect from them and (hopefully) where they are going as a company. That collective understanding must come from the entrepreneur/owner or senior executive.

This necessarily assumes a customer focused, alignment committed business owner with time to spend on the perceptions of each company he or she serves and understanding and gaining buy-in from employees. Unfortunately, as companies age and hopefully grow, the amount of effort required to accomplish the goals above becomes more daunting. Therefore various parts of these entrepreneurial responsibilities must necessarily be pushed down the organization.

Gotta Know Who We Are and What We Do

I know that sounds kind of silly but consider the fact that business owners lose track of the types of clients they have and even the market segments they serve. How does that happen? In the imperative to sell more and drive more revenue, many businesses become less discerning about to whom they sell, to what end and which markets or industries are at the core of initial success. I can say this with authority because I have from time to time fallen into the same trap.

So if our responsibility as business owners is to clearly state our goals, the path to achieving them, then gain alignment with our employees, we have to revisit our strengths, weaknesses and those practices that have yielded positive (or negative) results over the course of the company's existence.

Interestingly enough, at ACUMEN Corporation when we are first introduced to a new potential client company we spend a great deal of time in a process called "discovery". That term was first used by the legal profession as a way to describe the process of gathering data before a legal proceeding can begin whether it be a civil or criminal matter. In the past 20 years or so the term has come to represent the analytical process a consulting firm or software company employs to determine what makes a company tick and identify points of pain. As painful as it may seem, it may serve today's entrepreneur well to turn the focus inward and have a look at what works and what doesn't before undertaking the process of applying the metrics and repetitive processes it will take to define and execute a sustainable business plan.

In researching this chapter I found an interesting online article by Ken Burgin and Elizabeth Walker of The Marketing Masters that adds credence to my suggestion above. In part it says:

> *"A good first step in getting to the next level in your business is to 'discover' what your company is really good at. In business lingo, this is called 'defining your core competency', and it's often surprising that many business owners have never nailed this down.*

I think that is spot on. You need to find your core competency and work forward from there. That said, to grow your business you may need to apply the techniques and processes that have worked for you to new or extended market segments.

Your Personal Work Session

During our last jam session (our writers work session you will recall), Dan and I worked through an exercise using my company as a rough model. I'm going to ask Dan to pick up our discussion at this point and discuss how the business owner can examine the business as it is and add not only vision but metrics to the next steps and processes to achieve results.

Dan?

Thanks, Phil. I believe it would be helpful to provide a practical example of how to build linkage between the goals of the Owner/CEO and the foot soldiers, also known as sales people. This requires developing a step by step plan so that a sound linkage is made between a growth plan and critical territory level sales activities.

This effort starts with an analysis of where your revenue was sourced in the past, where your profit contributions within the revenue segments come from and are these trends and sources likely to continue. Also, where might there be new market/product areas where new growth will come from.

Since this is highly customized to the individual company, I'm going to take some poetic license and define some of those factors for a mythical company I will call Growth Unlimited (GU).

GU has been around for 10 years with modest growth until the last two years. Those years have shown a 20% growth in revenue each year. Not quite that much in profit but still pretty healthy at a 15% growth rate.

The company's revenues for 2017 are projected to be $10 million. GU manufactures conveyor belt systems used in multiple industries for companies that package and ship their products. $7M of the $10M comes from the consumer products Industry. 20% comes from commercial products companies and 10% comes from pharmaceutical companies.

The profit margins are 10% for consumer goods, 20% for commercial goods and 35% for pharmaceuticals.

As we develop this "linkage" exercise, we're going to identify a few of the factors that need to be considered at each level of management until we arrive at the desired sales activities needed to ensure the best opportunity to achieve the results GU CEO desires.

Organizational Linkage Roles:

Chief Executive Officer (CEO):

His view is that for a 5 year planning horizon, consumer products will continue to provide the majority of the revenue (over 50%). However, he would like to see a little better distribution to commercial products and especially pharmaceuticals.

Therefore, he sets a fairly aggressive revenue growth objective for 2019 of $12 million. He would like the contribution breakdown to be: consumer goods (8M), commercial goods (2.5M) and pharmaceuticals (1.5M).

With the end results and distribution defined, he then gives the respective general managers for each of the market segments the responsibility to further define where we might expect to achieve these numbers.

General Manager (GM):

After looking into the sources of the 2016 and 2017 revenue contributions from their market segments, general managers must now define customer and geographical makeup for their segment. This will enable the field sales executives to deploy their segment sales resources effectively.

The GM for the consumer goods market knows that the customers/prospects are fundamentally located in the Midwest. They provide a steady stream of revenue and moderate growth. Therefore, in order to grow this market by the 20% figure, his team must develop more east coast companies in 2018. He feels that this is best accomplished by focusing on the 20 largest east coast consumer products companies. To establish a "foothold" for 2018 and beyond, we need to penetrate four of them in 2018 with an average $100,000 of revenue from each of them.

The GM for the commercial products market determines that in order to have the best chance to achieve the results the CEO desires for 2018, she needs to lower the size of the target companies from $200M to $50M. A quick look at our database shows that this increases number of companies in that space to an additional 50. Her goal here is to close $50,000 or more of revenue in five of those larger companies in 2018.

The GM for the pharmaceutical market knows that it is made up of five or six mega large companies and as many as 100 medium-size ($100M or less) companies. These medium sized companies make decisions more quickly than their larger company brethren. Therefore, it's important to focus on these hundred companies and blanket them with a marketing and sales effort that closes at least $25K of business in 2018 from at least ten new companies. While this is clearly an aggressive growth in number of customers, the profit margin in this segment suggests we have to move quickly.

With this for segmentation, it's time to pass these objectives to the National Sales VP to develop an action plan to achieve the objectives given to him for 2018.

National Sales Manager:

Because of the different jargon, sizes, skills needed to effectively sell in the three market segments, if she decides to continue using three different sales teams to attack three different markets.

The **consumer** products sales team is made up of seasoned veterans who have experience in complex sales to multiple stakeholders.

Critical territory activity: Develop/monitor a detailed account plan with projected milestone dates throughout the year.

Measurement: Number of active account plans in assigned accounts as demonstrated in account reviews and milestone accomplishments.

> **Results:** 3-4 large transactions $300K to $750K per sales rep per year.

The **commercial** products sales team has younger sales reps who are used to dealing with multiple customers rather than one or two.

Critical territory activity: Marketing/networking focus using multimedia and association participation to open doors into targeted companies.

Measurement: Number of new contacts/meetings made per quarter in targeted accounts.

> **Results:** 6-8 transactions $75K to $150K per sales rep per year.

The **pharmaceutical** sales team is populated by the newest sales reps who are highly active and have a rigorous prospecting culture necessary to determine quickly what their best opportunities are for the coming year.

Critical territory activity: Conduct mass marketing campaigns combined with cold calling leading to face to face meetings.

Measurement: Number of phone calls made plus number of first time face to face meetings.

> **Results:** 6 to 12 transactions $25k to $50K over 3-4 accounts per sales rep per quarter.

From this determination of the types of activities within each division, it is now time to hand off to the sales manager to determine the right level of activity and the right metrics to determine whether that activity is working for each of their respective divisions.

Market Segment Sales Manager:

The activities measured in each of the segments will, of course, vary because of the particular customer set to whom they are marketing and selling.

However, it is imperative to set a quantifiable targeted number of activities the sales reps are expected to deliver. So, for instance, in the consumer products division a key activity is to have a defined account plans with defined benchmark activities that need to be accomplished by certain dates throughout the year.

The consumer segment sales manager tells each salesperson they must have account plans for every one of their existing accounts in place by January 31, 2018 and the new targeted account plans in place by February 28 2018.

As one of his routine critical activities, the commercial segment sales manager might ask his salespeople for a targeted list of companies with the specific contact to meet with. The metrics for this might be to meet with at least 25% of their targeted contact list by the end of the first quarter.

The pharmaceutical segment sales manager might realize that in his segment it's much more about how to get through the entire prospect list. So, each of the sales people might have 50 pharmaceutical companies in their territory and their objective is to contact, assess and prioritize, by the end of the first quarter of 2018, which of those 50 have reasonable opportunities in 2018.

The discussion above is by no means complete but it is meant to show how, when sales people execute defined activities that have been linked to top level results, that effort yields a reasonable view of which actions have the best chance of achieving the results desired. And also which activities should be modified later. Because as is understood by the United States armed forces, "No plan survives first engagement with the enemy". However, the effort to develop a "battle a.k.a activity plan" that is linked to the ultimate desired results provides the best framework for adjusting that original plan as intermediate results may indicate the need for.

** it is critically important to maintain a frequency of review meetings at the sales rep level: Quarterly for Large Accounts, Monthly for Medium Accounts and Weekly for Small Accounts. Then, the results of these meetings should be summarized at least quarterly with the next higher management level.

Action Items for Chapter 6

- Start from where you are in your company:
  - CEO/Owner Role: Set a financial goal for the current year, if not already set. If not sure what it should be, make an informed guess.

  - General Manager Role: Breakdown CEO overall goal into segments pertaining to your company.

  - If High Level Sales Executive exists, establish the revenue goal for the appropriate segment sales managers.

  - Sales Executive/Manager Role: Determine critical behaviors and frequency to be measured for each segment.

- You now have the structure of a plan to guide and make in process adjustments for your salespeople that are synchronized to the overall company goals.

Chapter 7

By the Numbers; The Death of "hopium"

"...Conversion of proposal to close...will allow sales management to do a deep dive into a sales rep's process to see what is working and what is not with a high degree of specificity."

Paul Alves, CEO, AG Salesworks

I have to admit that I fell in love with that word "hopium". The first time I heard it used was during one of our jam sessions in preparation for our first book on the '*"Willing To Buy"*Framework'. Dan used it to describe the delusional behavior displayed by his IBM sales teams as they reviewed their pipelines during periodic sales meetings. I thought he had coined the term himself and quickly jotted it down for later use. Dan informed me that he had picked it up along the way and frankly couldn't remember the origin.

As is my way I began to research the darned word, curious to know what exactly it means (in a classic sense) and who first used it. I ran into a site on the internet called Wordnik who provided the following (fairly obvious) definition it picked up from Wiktionary:

"irrational or unwarranted optimism"

The word pops up now and again, usually in a political or sometimes religious context, but I was surprised that I had no success in tracking down the origin. So let's just get on to our "anti "hopium"" crusade.

If you read our first book you know that the '*"Willing To Buy"*Framework' and the processes associated with it are all about getting to the real truths driving the sales cycle (or as we prefer the buy cycle). Truth is the enemy of "hopium". Oh of course we want our sales teams to be hopeful and positive, but we don't want that hope to be unwarranted and certainly not irrational. After all, who enjoys working with an irrational sales rep?

So our goal as business owners and/or sales managers is to ferret out the opportunities that are *real* and likely to bear financial fruit. There are many theories about how to do that, what steps to take and what tools to use, of course. Let's spend a moment on one commonly used sales tool that offers tremendous potential to facilitate the process but comes with an unintended downside.

On CRM and other Deadly Acronyms

By now I'm sure you are aware that CRM stands for "Customer Relationship Management". In general CRM represents a software program or set of programs that allows you to:

- capture information about the prospects in the pipeline
- take and track appropriate actions
- remind you of next steps
- … and hopefully lead you to closing the business

CRM suites also allow you to track activities with the prospects that you (hopefully) turn into clients from "cradle to grave". Some include service modules so that you can track support and service activities once the deal is booked.

The very best CRM systems are "configurable" in the sense that steps along the journey of the sell/buy cycle can be defined and tracked using your sequencing and lexicon. None the less, almost all CRM systems used to facilitate sales suggest some sort of variation of the following:

- Find a lead
- Contact the suspect (not yet a prospect in the world of *"Willing To Buy"*)
- Engage in a needs analysis
- Determine qualification
- Formulate a value proposition (hopefully tailored to the actual needs of the potential client…we can hope!)
- Propose your solution
- Close the deal

Dan Schultheis and Phil Perkins

Does that sound about right for your organization? Again, whether you are selling forklifts or computer software, some variation of the above process is likely in play. We'll spend more time on this sort of model later in the chapter.

Before we discuss the shortcomings of CRM, let's take a look at another sales aid called "Sales Force Automation" (SFA). During our careers, Dan and I have used this sort of tool and spoken to the developers on several occasions. Recently I had the opportunity to discuss CRM and SFA with Matt Hartman, founder of a software development company in Findlay, Ohio called Tour de Force. After having spent a great deal of time perusing their website, I knew Matt had some innovative ideas about mating CRM and SFA to particular market segments. Matt graciously allowed me to borrow the following definition of Sales Force Automation from his website.

Sales Force Automation Defined

"The process of maximizing the efficiency of the repeatable processes a sales person performs.

This is achieved through the use of software to automate and streamline business tasks, including Account Management, Contact Management, Opportunity Management, Project Management, Sales Funnel or Sales Pipeline Management, Sales Activity Management, Sales Forecasting Analysis, Sales Team Performance Evaluation, and Quoting."

I thought that was a particularly complete definition of SFA, but wondered how it differed from CRM (…are you getting tired of acronyms yet? I guess I am!). Luckily the Tour de Force website and later Matt himself went on to discuss the differences.

What does Sales Force Automation have to do with CRM?

"Sales Force Automation is often used interchangeably with CRM, however, CRM does not necessarily imply Sales Force Automation or the automation of sales tasks.

Whereas CRM is the strategy used to manage the relationships you have with your customers and the software that you use to implement that strategy, SFA is the strategy used to drive efficiencies in your sales processes."

Ah yes, it all becomes clearer now. But if you look closely at the definitions of both CRM and SFA, you may notice that there is no particular focus on the qualification and disqualification steps associated with successful sales efforts. Of couse that's where we come in with the '*"Willing To Buy"* Framework'.If you refer back to the last page you will notice that the third step of the pro forma sales process is "determine qualification". In traditional CRM and/or SFA suites, this is represented as a single step and weighted accordingly. There is a trap in that and to illustrate that trap I'm actually going to refer to our own book, *"Willing to Buy"; A Questioning Framework for Effective Closing*. Indulge me if you will.

The Flaw in Factoring and Weighting in the Sales Process

For years sales managers have looked for an ideal way to determine the probability of closing specific deals and have applied a certain weight to where you are in the step-by-step process leading to the close.

Here's noted business blogger Dave Brock, president and CEO of Partners in EXCELLENCE, illustrating the inherent flaws in factoring sales probabilities:

> *"One of the most used forecasting methodologies [is] based on a 'weighted revenue' approach.*
>
> *This approach takes the sum of all opportunities in the pipeline, multiplying the revenue for each opportunity by a probability factor. This makes sense statistically, it's called expected revenue. For example, if you have a $100,000 sale and a 70% probability, the expected value of the sale is $70K—we know this from statistics. So what's the problem?*
>
> *The root of the problem is really in the way most organizations assess the probability factor. For most organizations, the*

Dan Schultheis and Phil Perkins

probability assigned is based on where you are in the sales process. For example, if you have qualified the opportunity, you might have a 25% probability; after you have completed discovery, you have 50%; after you have submitted a proposal, you have 75%; and after you have closed, you have 100%. Makes sense, as you go through the sales process, presumably you are improving your chances of winning the business. All perfectly logical—all perfectly meaningless. Yet, virtually every CRM system, virtually every forecasting methodology, relies on this approach."

That means that if there are four suppliers bidding for the same contract, all of whom are stepping through the process at roughly the same time, the sales managers of all four supplier companies may project a 75 percent chance of closing and the commensurate amount of revenue. In fact, if you imagine for a moment that three competitors perfectly execute all of the pre-prescribed steps along the sales journey, all will predict with certainty that they will win the deal. Three will definitely be wrong and maybe all four.

The '"*Willing To Buy*" Framework' applies a more directed and specific question-and-feedback approach to determining the probability that you may win the business. Since Dan knew his IBM sales teams were driven by "hopium", he quickly realized that he would have to begin to apply a more logical approach to qualifying (and equally if not more importantly disqualifying) prospects that the team advanced as closable business. And the '"*Willing To Buy*"' methodology had to move well beyond the factoring and predictive analysis associated with the sales tools of the day and the subjective approach taken by the sales representatives.

Over time, Dan was able to analyze the impact of the new methodology in mathematical terms and in a moment I'm going to ask him to discuss the results. However, I do want to point out that both Dan and I believe CRM and SFA suites can be extremely valuable tools in capturing critical information and assisting in keeping sales professionals on track. In our view, the '"*Willing To Buy*" Framework' provides a logical and productive overlay and discipline that can change ones mindset from "hopium" to reality.

I'm going to turn this back over to Dan who will offer up a unique "two view" discussion of how the '"*Willing To Buy*" Framework' can help companies more accurately predict sales results. There are as many opinions on how to slice and dice data as there are CRM/SFA suites of course but Dan will now address how various stakeholders may look at the sales pipeline on a ***transactional*** basis and in the ***aggregate***. Dan?

Thanks, Phil. Let's start with:

A Discussion of the positive impact of using the *"Willing To Buy"* Framework for the CFO and Sales Manager (SM) roles:

The WTB framework provides a process to "Discount/Factor" an opportunity from its top line revenue projection to whether or not this decision will be made and the business be won. Initially, you may say, that any given opportunity will either happen or not. This is true when looking at opportunities one at a time. But, if you are a CFO and looking for a financial projection from the sales team, a detailed view of whether individual opportunities will close or not, may not serve you well. It may be better for you to review only the total projected sales output from the sales team against your budgeted goals.

Whereas in the SM role, using the framework to review each opportunity may enable you to better diagnose any true problems that need to be corrected to improve your sales people's performance. This will provide a more objective view of which actions to take rather than using "only gut feel" in a trial and error approach.

With this in mind, I've chosen these 2 functions that exist in any organization (even though in some companies these functions may occur within the same person) that can use the WTB framework but to entirely different ends.

The fact is that in both roles, we factor/discount/hedge projected sales numbers. In most cases this is done subjectively in our minds based on our view of the credibility of the person(s) (usually the SM) making the projection. What WTB does is minimize these subjective "hedges" by using a more objective process.

Why, you say, would I want to do this? Well, because the more one can objectively quantify the existing process/approach being used, either consciously or subconsciously, the more accurate our resulting conclusions will be.

A CFO/Financial Officer's View:

As a CFO, one of my main inputs is what kind of revenue flow can I expect over a certain period of time to fund ongoing operations, marketing, production, etc. In most organizations, who have a salesforce, this is main source of that input.

If you talk candidly to any CFO, they will tell you that their confidence in the accuracy of projections/forecasts coming from this group is very low. This is usually based on their experience in counting on past forecasts.

So, when the CFO asks for and receives a sales projection from the sales team, they either consciously or subconsciously adjust the amount projected. This is essential because projections such as these are an important component for the future planning of covering operating costs, salaries and/or making investments for future payback. The more accurately the CFO can "guess/estimate" future revenue flow, the better able they are to plan without dramatically changing their plans along the way due to the erratic nature of sales projections.

However, there will always remain the tendency for the CFO to look more closely at individual transactions when trying to assess what the future looks like for closing sales and seeing revenue flow tick up. While this is a normal tendency, it should be remembered that reviewing individual transactions is meant to help the salesperson develop a strategy and tactics to close the business as effectively as possible. But, when an assessment of the likelihood of a total projected revenue amount is the purpose of the review, then factoring the odds on each transaction happening and using only the total amount of those "factored" transactions is one of the only ways to get a reliable view of what the "business" can expect.

"How can you say this?" you might ask. It's because of the statistically defined "law of large numbers".

Some companies, especially the very large ones, take a broader look at the sales pipeline using a variation of something called **"The Law of Large Numbers"**. Let's start this discussion with a classic definition of this "law".

> *"Statistical concept that larger the sample population (or the number of observations) used in a test, the more accurate the predictions of the behavior of that sample, and smaller the expected deviation in comparisons of outcomes. As a general principle it means that, in the long run, the average (mean) of a long series of observations may be taken as the best estimate of the 'true value' of a variable. In other words, what is unpredictable and chancy in case of an individual is predictable and uniform in the case of a large group."*

Well that is a mouthful. The premise as it relates to sales projections is that the business owner, CFO and Sales Manager may get a better feel for real future sales results by factoring and discounting the total of the entire pipeline at the sales team or even sales person level.

Bear with me as we explore this concept and how WTB can be used in conjunction with 'The Law of Large Numbers' to provide the CFO with predicted results she can count on.

What if, as CFO or executive responsible for finances, you could:

- Have a more reliable "hedge" than your current "guessing game"?
- Stop feeling "victimized" by a lot of ""hopium"" from your sales team?

- Do resource planning and hire in a way that does not put you at a future risk of reducing that resource level because the sales team missed its sales projections?
- Have an alternative way to assess how large the company sales team needs to be from one based on the "pleadings/excuses" of the sales manager(s) about not having enough salespeople?

A Sales Manager's View:

As a Sales Manager (SM), one of our duties is to provide a sales projection, either formally or informally, to the CFO for their financial planning process. However, this CFO projection is really of secondary importance to you. Why? Because your view of job "1" is to oversee the activities and ultimately the sales production of the salespeople on your team.

There are many, many books on leading/managing a sales team. They usually discuss either general or very specific models as to what to measure/question. Most state that, in your SM role, you should meet with (or review reports; provided you have an installed CRM/SFA) each salesperson on a predetermined frequency to check whether they are performing the required activities that should lead to closing sales. When it is found that a given salesperson is not performing these activities and also there is an unsatisfactory sales results performance, the SM institutes corrective actions. These actions try to address whether the problem is lack of required activities, sales ability, opportunity management, planning skills or, in some cases, lack of territory potential.

If your assessment and subsequent corrective actions do not produce sales results then you are faced with a decision of whether to keep coaching and counseling the salesperson or terminate him/her.

What if you could:

- Determine much earlier in the sales cycle that the probability is low of closing a specific opportunity?
- Stop committing sales, support and management time to constructing solutions and preparing proposals?

- Determine if precious sales time is wasted on opportunities unlikely to close?
- Have a better handle on how many salespeople are needed to achieve sales goals rather than thinking more will "do the trick"?
- Gain the confidence of the CFO and other executive management that you have the ability not only to lead the sales team but provide dependable sales projections/forecasts.

Now, for both roles, CRM/SFA systems have made an attempt to provide a framework for objectively "hedging" by allowing an organization to standardize the stages/activities in their company's typical sales cycle, then allowing them to assign a probability percentage based on a given opportunity being at a certain "activity" stage level.

Though this is at least a step in the right direction of objectifying the sales projection process, it is limited by the fact that (as we mentioned before) if two sales teams from competing companies are working on the same opportunity and have arrived at the same activity stage level; let's say the proposal stage, then both companies will project the same percentage of probability of closing the business; even though clearly both will not win the business.

By adding the WTB framework, we bring an important, but usually not considered, factor into the opportunity probability process. That is the human factors addressed by WTB that assesses whether all the pieces (pillars) are in place to ensure a decision will be made at the end of the sales cycle.

This additional WTB assessment factor is critical because as is stated by most organizations using CRM/SFA their biggest competitor, which usually appears only after proposal time, is a non (or deferred)-decision.

Including the WTB framework process into any existing CRM/SFA system will inevitably improve predictability since we reduce the likelihood that many opportunities will continue to get to the proposal stage without a decision being made.

The reason for this is that, when the WTB framework is applied by the sales manager to top sales opportunities, the activities dedicated to these opportunities that can't answer most or all of the WTB pillars, will be either stopped forever or deferred to a time when the pillars are in place from the prospect's perspective.

As you will see in the following discussion, the addition of the WTB framework to the already existing activity level factoring/discounting will positively impact the CFO, as well as the SM, "what Ifs" identified above. I'll turn it back over to Phil to illustrate this point.

Revisiting and overlaying the *"Willing To Buy"* Framework

Well Dan, as we stated in our first book; as well as reiterated here, '"*Willing To Buy*'" must come from what is in the prospect/buyer's mind not the salesperson's. The more we understand about what drives the buying decision for the prospect the better chance we have of closing the deal.

So, a more expanded view of probability is one in which the WTB pillars are addressed, then used to add an additional factoring percentage to the activity stage percentage. We have elected to illustrate those typical stages using a composite of several clients who use SalesForce as their CRM/SFA tool. A typical sales cycle may look very much as below.

SFA Typical Stages with typical probability percentages associated with them:

* **Initial Contact**	**10%**
* **First Meeting**	**20%**
* **Requirements Gathering**	**30%**
* **Proposal Given**	**40%**
* **Executive Presentation**	**50%**
* **Finalist**	**70%**
* **Contract Negotiations**	**80%**
* **Signed Contract**	**100%**

You will note that the first three steps fall into the category of data gathering or getting to know the prospect and what drives their willingness to buy a given product or service. It is in those first three critical stages that ‘*"Willing To Buy"*’ adds real value. This model presumes that if you get through the first three steps successfully, you should have a 30% probability of closing the deal. But whether you give yourself the "tick marks" associated with these stages, this presumption is usually very subjective and can be given to a "hopium" way of viewing probabilities.

In our view, what has occurred after most SFA systems are implemented is that the original percentage probability numbers associated with the Opportunity Funnel in the SFA system are ***rarely*** revisited after the initial assumed stage percentage listed in the implementation phase. This is true even though, invariably, the actual probability changes over time based on data input from the sales team's experience in managing and closing opportunities.

We feel that, based on our experience with dozens of users of SFA systems, a more realistic adjustment of these probability percentages would be to assign a 0% probability percentage to the stages before the proposal stage. And, that the proposal stage itself should have its percentage lowered significantly. From our analysis, we have found that the percentage probability for the proposal stage in most SFA implementation has historically been at best 25%. This means that the sales projections at this level could be as much as twice what the actual probability should be.

Therefore, it is our recommendation to most current and future SFA users that they revisit their imbedded probability percentages every six months and update the percentages based on their actual sales team track record.

Based on this discussion, the percentages in our example should start out conservatively as the following:

* **Initial Contact**   0%
* **First Meeting**   0%
* **Requirements Gathering**   0%

*	**Proposal Given**	**25%**
*	**Executive Presentation**	**40%**
*	**Finalist**	**50%**
*	**Contract Negotiations**	**80%**
*	**Signed Contract**	**100%**

Now, with this adjustment, the WTB Framework can be inserted, by sales management, as a percentage probability accelerator in adjusting the above numbers.

Here's how it might work. The '*"Willing To Buy"* Framework' itself is weighted. Each of the pillars (which remember represent the word(s) of the buyer NOT the salesman) has a value in terms of completing the WTB process. Here are those percentages:

- Justification Evident (JE)   20%
- Decision Cycle Clear (DCC)   20%
- Money Available (MA)   20%
- *"Willing To Buy"*(WTB)   40%

Once the '*"Willing To Buy"* Framework' questioning has begun at the first meeting with the prospect about the potential opportunity, the sales manager should review each specific opportunity she chooses with the sales representative. On an ongoing basis, and based on which pillars the salesperson has completed with his prospect's input, the associated above percentage(s) of the pillar(s) can be multiplied with the standard stage percentage, thus giving a new uplifted probability percentage. Also, these WTB Pillar uplift percentages would be carried through to uplift the later stage percentages for this opportunity; thus resulting in a new projected sales number for use in the forecasting roll up to the CFO.

Here's an example of how the additional uplift might impact a single opportunity probability in the pipeline. Suppose only MA and JE factors above have been satisfied through interaction with the prospect. In this scenario, the adjusted probability at the proposal stage would become

35% (25% + (25% x 40%)). This would then change the succeeding stage percentages by the same 10% for this opportunity, as follows:

*	**Initial Contact**	**0%**
*	**First Meeting**	**0%**
*	**Requirements Gathering**	**0%**
*	**Proposal Given**	**35%**
*	**Executive Presentation**	**60%**
*	**Finalist**	**80%**
*	**Contract Negotiations**	**90%**
*	**Signed Contract**	**100%**

As we have pointed out on more than one occasion, this additional layer of qualification can seem daunting at first but once implemented for a sales team within the SFA system, it becomes routine. Consider the following:

You will note that once the initial steps of the typical SFA model have been completed, a proposal is submitted. The word "submitted" undersells and undervalues that step. As we all know, proposals can be large and even very technical documents often prepared by experts. And more often than not those experts are not the salesperson.

With that in mind the WTB framework plays a critical role. In our view, and particularly when many prospects are in our pipeline, the sales representative should routinely earn the right to commit resources to a particular prospect's proposal. '"*Willing To Buy*" 'takes the guesswork out of that process and, because the sales manager insists that the pillars be addressed by the salesperson from the very first meeting, the inherent disqualification philosophy of WTB reduces the potential that an opportunity will make it to the "resource burning" proposal stage.

Phil, let me just add something if I may. After reviewing the above material, one might also conclude that this double factoring using both types of probabilities (Stage and Pillar) might be too rigorous. This is where the idea of "hopium" must be taken into consideration. That is, the addiction that salespeople and, to a great extent, sales management have that is subconsciously affecting their subjecive judgement is strong.

Accurate forecasts are not just **nice to have** but they are, for most organizations, a **have to have.**

Accurate forecasts in a business are necessary so that the future can be more clearly anticipated and thereby provide a more realistic input to executive management/ownership on which to base the decision to make future investments and/or add resources.

So, quite simply, allowing Hopium to exist while trying to close a specific opportunity with a prospect is not bad. It can keep the salesperson hanging in there and competing longer. But, when it comes to forecasting to the business (a.k.a. upper management), there is very little room for "hopium". In other words, an accurate forecast that predicts what actually will happen is infnitely more valuable than an overly optimistic forecast that makes everyone happy when it is given but is useless for business planning when that forecast is missed.

Good points, Dan. And of course if the '"*Willing To Buy*" Framework' is applied on a transactional level, then the Law of Large numbers approach used by larger firms with bigger pipelines is far more meaningful. Sure the CFO may take a little convincing about the new probability model. And yes he or she may do a little factoring themselves, but overall the revenue projections will be more realistic and reliable.

Action Items for Chapter 7

- Using the list from the Chapter 4 exercise, perform the following steps:

    - Subtotal the sales dollars associated with each opportunity at a given sales cycle step and then multiply it by the probability percentage you established in the last step.
    - Finally calculate the two totals:

        1. The "list price" total of all the sample sales opportunities in all of the steps of the sales cycle.
        2. The "discounted/factored" total of all the sample sales opportunities in all of the steps of the sales cycle.

- Now is the time to assess your "dead proposal" volume. To do that:

    - Count the number of opportunities that currently are at the proposal stage.
    - Additionally, if they are available, count the opportunities in the last six months that are no longer in your opportunity funnel but made it to the proposal stage. Add up two totals: 1. those proposals that have closed in the last six months and 2. those that did not close but remained stuck at the proposal stage.
    - If the number of proposals that did not close in the last six months is more than 50% of the total number of proposed on opportunities, then you have a significant potential for saving both selling and proposal preparation resources by using the WTB framework as described in this chapter to remove the "disqualified, a.k.a. unlikely to close" opportunities earlier rather than later and thus save significant time and resources.

Note; Based on the above process in this exercise, if you guide your salespeople to reach for 100% of your factored revenue goal (both Stage and WTB Factoring), you will almost always meet or exceed your annual objective.

Chapter 8

Are They *"Willing To Buy"* From ME?

"...People don't buy from people they like, they buy from people they trust".

IEC commercial web site

While both Dan and I do a great deal of research as we write about business and in particular the business of selling, it isn't often that I Google a subject and find myself on a commercial website and rapidly becoming a fan of how the company presents itself. But that's exactly what happened with I encountered www.iecdelivers.com the website of a "Sign, Graphics and Digital Imaging Solutions" company based in California.

Our friend Charlie Green of the *Trusted Advisor*, who wrote the foreword for our first book together, often reminds us that good business decisions and interactions are based on mutual trust.

To frame the discussion, here's a quote directly from his blog and the foreword to *"Willing To Buy"; A Questioning Framework for Effective Closing*:

> *"I've always believed in my own work on integrating sales and trust that the best sales are those which are first and foremost*

of benefit to the customer, and only then also of benefit to the seller. Most sales books (and most salespeople) approach sales from the zero-sum point of view, the competitive strategy point of view, in which one plus one always equals something very close to two, and selling is about transferring funds from the wallet of the buyer to the wallet of the seller. It is precisely this attitude which has led to such a bad reputation for the field of sales."

Clearly the folks at IEC agree so I'm going to kick off this chapter by quoting from the IEC website.

"It is often said that customers buy from people they like. While we don't usually buy from people we dislike, there is one more dimension to this old saying.

Customers buy from people they trust."

IEC follows that overall positioning of their company focus with a fairly detailed overview of how they would proceed with the pre-sales engagement should their firm be selected. The "go to market" strategy at IEC is very impressive and I encourage you to visit their site and read more.

But building mutual trust can be a challenge, can't it? After all, you have to actually "get in the door" before you can begin to build that trust. Clearly the folks at IEC want you to understand right up front that they expect to have to earn your trust. (There's that word "earn" again…I like it).

I give IEC high marks in creativity in that they position themselves as both a *potential* trusted advisor and even "thought leader" by using the words of a noted expert (CJ Ng) to paint a picture of who they are as a company and how their sales team is different. Moreover, the verbiage gives you an idea of what the "buying experience" might be.

Of course the '*"Willing To Buy"* Framework' doesn't deal directly with prospecting, cold calling or demand generation. It **does** deal directly with building trust via the human touch of asking good, well-conceived questions and showing that you really care about the answers. What IEC and other "smart" organizations have done is put themselves in a position to do just that.

"Willing To Buy" and the Trust Equation

Think about this for a moment. (Bear with me as this may seem a tad obvious) Imagine you are at social gathering or convention and engaged in conversation with a new acquaintance. If that person asks you questions about how *you* feel about a given subject and gives you time to respond - perhaps even nodding in agreement and asking follow-up questions - does that make you feel good? If they spend most of the conversation telling you about their company or their kids or the new boat almost to the exclusion of finding out more about you, does that tend to be a deal breaker in terms of forming a long term relationship? Most people have experienced both scenarios and rarely do the results differ.

Some time ago during a "jam session" (our terminology for writing strategy sessions) we invited my partner and company CFO Sandra Dube to join in the discussions. We often call the '*"Willing To Buy"* Framework' "the sales methodology that even a CFO can love" and in no small part it is because of the reaction Sandra had to the concepts contained therein.

During that session, Sandra pointed out that the framework did a great job of qualifying a buyer as *"Willing To Buy"* **something.** But she wondered out loud how it proved the buyer would buy from the seller who used the framework. Great question. Got the answer. The framework positions the seller as someone who isn't seeking to win the battle, isn't seeking to prevail but to facilitate the process of buying something that adds demonstrable value to the buyer. When done properly, the buyer has a clearly defined path to make a good decision and the seller can tell (in addition to the obvious willingness to buy) the following:

- Whether the buyer has a real need and can define it in business terms
- Whether the need is immediate

- The consequences of not addressing that need
- ......and whether the product or services represented by the sales professional can meet that need.

If the sales person looks at each interaction as an opportunity to deliver value (even if only advice) to the prospect, trust tends to build. And if people buy from people they trust...well you know the rest.

In terms of the research that goes into formulating informed, trust building questions, you might want to refer to the first book where we identify certain data available on the internet as "tells that sell". Using the methods mentioned therein can rapidly build credibility if and when you have the opportunity to discuss opportunities with your prospect.

Dan has a great perspective on trust based selling and many stories of success thanks to the proper execution of the '"*Willing To Buy*"Framework' and I'll turn it over to him at this juncture for further thoughts. Dan?

Phil, thanks for tackling what can be a confusing and elusive concept about how a salesperson can build trust in the prospect.

I'd like to piggy back on your discussion from a different psychological point of view. And, if I may, I'd like to introduce this point of view by quoting an excerpt from a blog from our friend Charles Green. The title of the blog is:

Clients Don't Buy Solutions, They Buy Problem Definitions

And here's an excerpt from that powerful blog topic:

> "*The client doesn't buy the best solution: instead, they reward the firm that did the best job of helping them define the problem. You're not getting paid to do the job – you're getting rewarded for having created the best ah-ha for the client – the ah-ha that says, 'Ah, yes – that is indeed precisely the issue that we've been having all along here. That's the heart of the matter.'*

Having gotten that ah-ha, why in the world would a customer then hire someone else to deliver on the vision you've jointly created? Why would you trust anyone but the ones who created the bond with you to develop the insight to actually get you over the river? You just wouldn't, that's all.

Clients don't buy value: they buy the people they have come to trust. In particular, they hire those who have helped them define their problem in a way that they can finally see their way clear to a resolution of their issues. The project, the sale, is not 'the thing' – it is simply the currency of reward for having best-defined the problem."

Now, from my own experience in developing, using and teaching the *"Willing To Buy"* Framework', I've realized that it builds trust in a very subtle but powerful way. To illustrate this, let me talk about how all of us go about finding solutions to problems; both personally and professionally.

First of all, at any given time we all have multiple priorities and a myriad of problems that are vying for our attention to be solved. Depending on our time available and the urgency of the problem to be solved, one or another of our problems take priority in our consciousness. As we know, though, in day to day living, these urgencies and priorities ebb and flow depending on what other issues are also vying for our attention.

With the rapid pace that we must operate in today, we are usually pressured to solve problems quickly. To facilitate rapid solutions, most of us define the problem but quickly move to what attributes and features a solution should have. Once we have those initial attributes (aka requirements) we tend to be consumed by the solution and, in many cases, lose sight of the original problem.

"Why is this a problem", you might ask. Because, if the solution has multiple attributes and we do not keep a clear link to the issues associated with the problem, we may wind up picking a solution based on an attribute that isn't critical to the original problem.

The '"*Willing To Buy*" framework' helps prospects keep the problem/ solution linkage absolutely clear by using a gentle questioning approach around the 4 pillars of the WTB framework. The WTB pillar enables them to reflect on their personal motivation of why solving this problem is important. The JE pillar aids them in solidifying any "business case" they can use to prove the need for a solution. The MA pillar allows them to predetermine whether they have allotted enough funding and resources to actually implement the solution. And, finally, The DCC pillar guides them in preconditioning all parties that need to say yes to the proposed solution. What we have helped our prospects do, just as Charlie said in his blog, we have "...*have helped them define their problem in a way that they can finally see their way clear to a resolution of their issues* ".

The reason this approach is so powerful in getting prospects to buy from us is that it uses the same questioning process that effective psychologists use. The good ones don't give us the answer but continually ask us reflective questions until we have our own "Ah-Ha" about our problem and its solution. I would also add that for those of us who have had a successful experience with a psychologist who has helped us in this way, we would not seek another psychologist to help us with future problems; even if they had a lower fee.

So, likewise, the use of the '"*Willing To Buy*" Framework' is a gentle, compassionate, and effective form of helping other human beings reflect and ultimately ensure that not only are they solving the right problem, but also that the problem has the urgency for that person to put their efforts into finding and implementing a solution.

Thus, trust is formed as a solid by-product of the WTB framework.

So let's finish up by taking a look at a real-life story of how the utilization of the '"*Willing To Buy*" Framework' can build trust and thereby help to close a key deal. This is based upon my work managing sales teams at IBM of course but the concepts are transferable.

As you may recall, I was a "marketing manager" for IBM in Indianapolis and responsible for a sales team of seven representatives. In addition to

Dan Schultheis and Phil Perkins

managing the group and forecasting the business monthly that my team would close, I was also responsible for assisting my reps to close business where I thought I could help.

One of my successful reps, let's call him Larry, was trying to sell the 1st National Bank of Indiana an IBM System running IBM's Banking Application Software. Larry thought he had done all the work necessary to close the business but couldn't get the bank president to buy the system.

I had reviewed Larry's WTB spreadsheet for this prospect and watched him get answers to some of the pillars over the last few weeks. However, he was having a particularly difficult time finding out the WTB pillar from the president. You will recall that the WTB pillar deals with personal justification to make a decision. I thought I could help him with this so I asked him to set up an appointment with the president.

After synchronizing calendars, we were able to meet. In the meeting, Larry began to review what he had found out from the president and his staff about justification (JE), budget & resources (MA), and who was involved in the decision (DCC). The president was key to our getting the business. However, I noticed that, as my rep reviewed the previous items, the president seemed somewhat interested but not enthusiastic enough to make a decision now.

I decided to address my perception with the president; after all it's better to know sooner rather than later whether he was ready to make a decision. So, my observational question to him was, "Mr. Conrades, I've noticed that you seem to agree with what Larry has reviewed today but my impression is that, for some reason, you don't seem ready to get behind this decision".

To my surprise, he said, "Well, your perception is correct. I appreciate all of Larry's effort but I need to think about this for a while". I thanked him for his candor but decided that before I left I would try to find if he had any WTB pillar motivation to make this decision.

I asked him, "If you don't make this decision for the next six months, what would be the impact on your bank?" Mr. Conrades said that the bank definitely needed to upgrade its current system but his hesitation was that it seemed that they have had to upgrade their system every two years and he wanted to know what IBM and my team could do to make sure that didn't happen this time.

I thought a moment how to respond to his question because if I asked the right question now, I could get a handle on whether or not there was a WTB energy for him. He had been an IBM customer for several system upgrades in the past. So, I told him that now, as in the past, we sized the system based on his growth projections and the configuration would last him as long as his bank's growth did not exceed the volumes he gave us. So, I said, "If you guarantee us that your bank will not grow over the next two years more than your estimate, our proposal will handle it".

He immediately said, "I won't give you any such guarantee". I said, "I didn't think so. That's because it's your past growth success that has brought us here. You've been directing your bank's success and exceeding it. I humbly suggest that is the root of your frustration and, more importantly, should be a source of pride for you".

He looked at us for a moment, then said, "I've had many of your competitors calling on me but none has asked me the questions that Larry has about the justification (JE), money & resource requirements (MA) and decision-making team (DCC). And, now, the last piece just fell into place for me from your question. Until I realized I was driving the growth, I was suspicious of all technology vendors. I thought you all just wanted to sell me on something. Now, I realize why I should want to grow out of my system every two years. It's because I'll always be exceeding my growth goals (WTB)".

Mr. Conrades said, "Give me the contract and let's get on with this installation. And, by the way, you, and your team, are the only vendor that took the time to look at this problem from my point of view. And, because of that, I trust your recommendation above all others".

As we drove back to the office, Larry and I gave each other a "high five" because of two things; first, we got the order and second, we saw that WTB cut through the clutter and quickly establish the prospect's trust.

So, you can see that the time and effort put into implementing the '"*Willing To Buy*" Framework' paid off for the customer, for Larry, for me and for IBM.

It's Phil again and have to say I love that story. However, as Dan shared it with me during one of our planning sessions, I could visualize how Larry squirmed as Dan asked the hard questions and pressed the president for the "reality" of the situation. But Dan knew that if he framed his questions and comments in the right way he would free the president up to talk about the real motivators.

I have been on sales calls with my team where I "pulled a Columbo". If you recall that old detective series, Columbo would often feign being behind the information curve and ask the suspect to forgive him for asking seemingly ill-advised questions. The technique caused the other party to talk about issues in a different and more transparent way…at least in the series. That technique often works as in Dan's story even if it makes the sales representative a little uncomfortable! Hey, it worked with suspects so why not prospects?

Action Items for Chapter 8

- Develop a list of your most loyal customers; the more the better but at least 10.
- Now, develop an additional list of prospects (10) that decided for your competitor or didn't make a decision.
- The CEO/Owner/Highest Level Sales Executive should perform this step:

  - Meet with all 20 of the companies compiled in the last two steps and ask the Loyal Customers what attributes of your company make them so loyal to You.
  - Ask the no- buying prospects what attributes could you improve on in the future to win future business –

- Finally summarize the two groups.

The results will almost always demonstrate that loyal customers voice their trust that your company has their best interest at heart and the non-buying prospects will talk about your product features and/or prices.

Conclusion: If you can replicate how your sales team handled the loyal customers and apply that technique to all new customers and prospects your loyal base will grow robustly (The WTB framework provides management as well as salespeople with a vocabulary that generates trust because all questions are framed around what is in the best interest of the customer).

Chapter 9

Of Rigor and Results

"The long and short of it is, we need more rigor in all kinds of programs."

Margaret Spellings, Former Secretary of Education

Over the course of writing two books on the '*"Willing To Buy"* Framework, Dan and I have been discussing the power of crafting the right types of questions and really listening to the answers (as Dan did in the story from chapter eight). Our fear has been that the casual reader will think *"of course good questions matter and, hey, I'm a good listener"* and leave it at that. We all hope that we can frame a problem well and propose a good solution but more often than not we fall back into the old "I've heard all this before and I can sell you a solution" mode.

Certainly, that approach worked for many sales representatives over the years. After all, the buyers garnered most of their information about the needed product or service from the salesperson themselves. They could then believe them or not and buy from the one that was **most** credible or at least believable.

But here are a couple of <u>certainties</u> in today's marketplace. In all cases. the prospect knows much more about their particular and often unique problems and goals than the sales person does, no matter how long he or she has been in the business. Moreover, before allowing a sales representative in the door most prospects will have scoured the Internet finding out as much about the salesperson's company and product(s) than could reasonably be covered in two demonstrations or executive briefings.

With the above in mind, it leads one to realize that, while many competitive products or services on the face may adequately address the problems and needs of a prospect, the approach to problem definition plays a much greater role today in terms of differentiation. Thus, the need to practice the art of questioning on a routine basis.

Another (blankety blank) Sports Analogy

Okay. I apologize profusely, but during our conversations about the need for coaching in the sales profession Dan and I keep coming back to sports. Virtually all sports require rigor for athletes to excel. Ballplayers may be blessed with natural ability and drive, but almost all would tell you that doing what they do over and over again and fine tuning the process is what boosted them from "good to great".

As we write this book, the New England Patriots stand as a perfect example of the analogy. They have won multiple Super Bowls and have done it with a band of "good" players with only one or two real superstars. More on that in a minute. Almost to a man they would tell you they won as a team with each man contributing in his own unique way and doing one specific job well.

In professional football, there are coaches for everything. From the head coach, down to what are called position coaches, all have the job of instilling football "best practices" into each player. Now I'm no Bill Belichick fan. I find his press conferences annoying and condescending. Many do. (Hey that's completely beside the point but I had fun putting it on paper.)

But Bill Belichick will be first ballot Hall of Fame inductee because he knows how to drive home the techniques and discipline that yield consistent winners. If a player doesn't readily grasp a concept, Belichick is a master of using all his tools to illustrate the wisdom of "doing it his way…the way of the Patriots".

Again, Coach Belichick doesn't have a core of superstars, but one of those players most would agree has been Tom Brady (still playing as we go to press). But consider this. He was a sixth-round draft choice. A man who many say will be remembered as the greatest quarterback of all time even had a difficult time choosing between baseball and football. Even so, Belichick saw something in the young recruit and began teaching him the basic differences in quarterbacking on the college level and as part of the National Football League.

Most sportswriters agree that there might not have been a Brady without a Belichick. Both might have still had good careers in the NFL, but Brady's talent bolstered by Belichick's patient yet insistent coaching style combined to fire up a multiple Super Bowl winning team.

Building a Winning Sales Team

Of course, there is no Super Bowl for sales teams. Oh there may be awards banquets, bonuses and "attaboys" (…and who knows…maybe trophies or plaques…) depending upon the company, but the real payoff comes in gaining the ability to close deals consistently and build customer satisfaction without fail.

So, let's discuss techniques that a sales manager or business owner might use to "coach" sales representatives from good to great using the '*"Willing To Buy"* Framework'. As a football team will do as much research on the next opponent as possible, so should the sales leader gather as much data about the prospect as possible to "frame" the sale. In the first book we discuss "Tells that Sell". Much information about a prospect company and often key owners or managers can be gleaned from the Internet. But often certain information is purposely obscured.

I'm going to suggest an important question about a prospect or clients that I have often asked my sales professionals and even consultants over the years. It is perhaps a bit controversial. Is it "profiling or perspective"? The question I ask is "how old do you think the prospect is?". I know that we are predisposed to try to make that statistic irrelevant, but everyone from television producers to cosmetic companies aim at demographics. Why should your company (or mine) be any less direct in reaching out to various age groups?

In my case, it is a matter of the perspective of the project decision maker(s). A 30 year old CFO grew up learning about and using much different tools than a 55 year old CEO. They ask different questions much of time, building upon the body of knowledge they have built up during their education years, no matter how extensive (or limited). The 30 year old is very likely to rely on the Internet where some (not all) buyers over 50 or 55 might defer to suggestions and referrals from friends and colleagues. There are no absolutes in this area. Some seniors are tech savvy and some millennials may have less interest in internet marketing due to other external factors. But in general, like groups buy in like ways.

So, I often try to gain perspective by asking about age, sometimes about any signs that the decision makers supports any particular university or college, if they are involved in certain charities and even if they are veterans. After all, most veterans are very focused on doing a job correctly and quickly. They can bring discipline to the buying process and knowing about that background allows the sales representative to be prepared.

The Internal Questioning Framework

In both of our books regarding the '*"Willing To Buy"* Framework', we have spent a great deal of time discussing how the sales representative can ask the right kinds of questions to get to the reality of a deal. With practice this sort of "discovery" becomes second nature. Alas, many sales managers and *business owners fail to realize that part of their job is to ask equally well-conceived and pointed* questions of their sales team.

Let's take this a bit further and discuss an example of how a sales manager might approach digging a bit deeper. In the pillar called Decision Cycle Clear (DCC) a sales person would be framing the question around who would be involved in the decision-making process. Once the sales representative comes back to the office and attends a sales meeting, the dialogue might go something like this.

For the sake of this example let's say that Larry, our sales rep yet again, is calling on Ben the warehouse manager at the Jerry Rigger Company who are in the market (he thinks) for a new coordinated warehouse forklift system. Let's say that Larry's manager is Paul. Borrowing from the prior section, let's say that it has been established that Ben is a 41 year old mid-manager with Jerry Rigger.

Paul: *Well Larry this Rigger looks like a pretty good prospect. I see that you met with Ben. He's the warehouse manager.*

Larry: *Yes, and I think he is very impressed with our company and offering. This feels like a solid deal.*

Paul: *And is Ben the ultimate decision maker?*

Larry: *Well, I mean, he's the warehouse manager and will oversee the use of the system, so I would think so.*

Paul: *Has he mentioned anyone in upper management by name?*

Larry: *Oh yes, he did mention Mark who is his boss, but just in passing.*

Paul: *So, what it Mark's title?*

Larry: *Ummm…director of operations I think?*

Paul: *Did Larry mention needing Mark's approval for the funds?*

Larry: *He said he would need to "run it by him", but it seemed like he could make the decision and just go for funding.*

Paul: *Did he say that in his own words?*

Larry: *No not exactly. Should I go back and ask?*

Paul: *I think that would be a good idea. Also, you mention "go for funding", is this budget not yet approved?* (…to the reader, Paul is jumping to the MA or Money Available Pillar now given the little "tell" that Larry doesn't really know if money is allocated. Paul is astute enough to understand that a piece of the puzzle is missing).

Larry: *I guess I didn't ask that question specifically.*

Paul: *It's always a good idea to establish that as early in the process as possible. Since you have to circle back to find out more about who is part of the decision and if money is there for the project, I suggest you spend a bit of time thinking about how you can frame the questions. That way Ben feels as though you are simply trying to help him move forward on getting what he needs in his warehouse.*

This is a very simple example of the rigor associated with getting to the reality of a sales opportunity with a well-meaning sales representative. It takes some time and patience to help sales professionals understand the importance of this sort of exercise. The '*"Willing To Buy"* Framework' helps to establish guidelines for the needed rigor.

Dan, I wonder if you can add some suggestions on how the sales manager or business owner can be consistent in the "internal questioning framework".

Sure, Phil, I'll be glad to. But before we get into some of the rigorous questions a sales manager might ask to help the salesperson understand what it means to "know" the WTB pillar has been covered, I'd like to talk a bit about how to keep salespeople sufficiently motivated so they thoroughly understand whether or not a given WTB pillar has been has been completed for a given prospect.

I want to do this by quoting Dr. Wallace Johnston, former professor at Virginia Commonwealth University and radio personality, or as he was affectionately known, "Dr. Wally". He had a very clear and firm position on the subject of motivating others. His beliefs in this area are:

1. **Motivation (internal) = Motive (internal) + Action (internal)** – Internal motivation is a combination of two distinct internal factors; the first is our own motive for accomplishing any goal and the second is action based on that motive. However, since most of us are not very good at the self-discipline (as Phil said earlier "rigor") and therefore we need to move to belief number 2.

2. **Rules (external) + Compliance (external) → Habit (new behaviors)** – to build a foundation for the motivation to change, an external resource (e.g. sales manager) must put rules in place and then insist on compliance to these rules over time by "inspecting the salespeople's WTB answers". This will lead over a period of time belief number 3.

3. **Habit + Reinforcement + Time = Effectiveness** – if these habits are reinforced consistently and continually over time, effectiveness of the process (e.g. WTB) will be demonstrated to the people (e.g. salespeople). Which will finally lead to belief number 4.

4. **Effectiveness + Results = Motivation** – once the effectiveness is proven by the required action of the salespeople, the results will come and this will result in the internal motivation to keep doing the behaviors (e.g. the WTB pillar questioning) being achieved.

<u>Conclusion: "Motivation isn't something inspired on the front-end of the process by management but rather a result on the back-end of a management compliance process".</u>

What this explanation says is that it is incumbent upon all of us in our role as sales managers to ensure that we put the proper rigor/compliance in place and consistently execute it with our salespeople. By doing this we enable the sales people to imbed the '*"Willing To Buy"*' approach into their muscle memory and sales DNA.

This is a duty we cannot shy away from because as we all know salespeople, like most of us, are poor self-managers when it comes to modifying their habits (a.k.a. sales approach). We must ensure that the WTB system is a learned by our team. The optimal way to do this is to insist that they prove to us that they understand the WTB framework properly by answering our questions about their execution of WTB pillar with their prospects.

With this in mind, here are some examples of questions a sales manager could ask to ensure the salespeople are uncovering if the WTB pillars exist for identified prospect(s):

"Willing To Buy"

- Are the decision makers (your current contact plus others involved in the decision) *"Willing To Buy"*, in their minds?
- Why is this so from the prospect's perspective?
- What is the evidence that this is so? - Verbal assurance, impending event, upper management insistence?
- Who are the others involved in the decision who also must be *"Willing To Buy"* for this proposition to go forward?

Justification Evident

- Is the justification evident in the minds of all who are involved in this decision?
- What is that justification? (Note: Be aware that the prospects will probably give the salesperson an intangible or non-quantified reason at first but the salesperson must try to prevail, if possible, to help their prospect quantify the dollar effect on the business)
- What is the time period over which the savings will be realized?
- Is there more than just one area in which this project will save the prospect company money?

Money Available

- Is there a budgeted amount for this project? If not, how might funds be appropriated to complete this project?
- Is the money for this project in your contact(s)' control or must he/she go to higher management to allocate funds for this effort?
- What is the breakdown of the projected costs and allocations of the funds?
  (e.g. product, software, services, training, etc)?
- What is the flexibility to go for more funds if the solution warrants it?

Decision Cycle Clear

- What is the sign-off path through management once the salesperson's primary contact agrees with their recommendation?
- Are there "hidden" parties who may need to be sold separately (e.g. committee, "silent" partner, whoever holds the purse strings, etc.)?
- Is it appropriate for the salesperson to go either with their contact or separately to the "other" parties to make the case for the solution?
- The salesperson must ask the prospect, in summary for this pillar after the prospects questions have been answered, "What else could keep this project from moving forward?"

The above questions are merely a starting point for the sales manager to inspect each salesperson's understanding and adoption of the WTB framework. Each of you, as sales managers, will add to these questions over time with your own "spin" on helping the salesperson realize whether they have identified a given **WTB** ® pillar.

Though this process does have rigor and demands the sales manager's commitment to "compliance" from their sales team, the effectiveness of execution will come as will predictable positive sales results.

Chapter 10

Okay...what's next?

"The first step toward change is awareness. The second step is acceptance."

Nathaniel Branden

You will notice that this will be a very short final chapter. I could have written this as an epilogue. However, I am told that very few people read introductions, forewords, or epilogues. So, I'm using this little trick to hold your attention.

First of all, let me tell you that Dan and I have enjoyed writing the *"Willing To Buy"* books immensely. Our dialogue, both live in our conference room and that portrayed in the books, is spirited, and thought provoking. Many years ago, Dan formulated the *'"Willing To Buy"* Framework' and put it into practice at IBM with stellar results. At the time we met, I ran an IBM partner firm. As readers of both books already know, I was an "early adopter" of this powerful sales tool.

Now for a dose of reality. I have spoken with a number of "sales professionals" both the kind still carrying a bag (by choice or not) and the kind managing sales teams. Without actually reading our books I was offered up the old *"hey things have changed...sales isn't the same...people shop differently"*. In other words, *"hey Phil and Dan, how could a book about a sales tool have any relevance today?"*.

But I'm a business owner. I have to make decisions on how to invest my hard-earned money every day. In the modern world, one must invest in a company's web presence, Search Engine Optimization (SEO), CRM (we've already discussed that) and the personnel to carry out ever more specialized tasks. What I don't want to invest money in is wasted time. After all these years in management I have no tolerance for over-inflated pipeline reports. I cannot afford to have sales representatives investing their time (paid for by my company's money) in deals that are not fully qualified.

Qualification has almost nothing to do with gut feel. Dan and I have both sold deals valued in the millions of dollars. We have met with "C-Level" executives in companies large and small. I think both of us are damned good salesmen. On the other hand, we have both been fooled by our "gut feel" that a deal would close. We have been fooled by claims of "you've got this", by invitations to golf outings, to lunches at the club and the list could go on.

The *"Willing To Buy"* books never claimed to address "demand generation". It won't help find suspects. That's where the new processes and technologies play best. Sure, we need lots of leads to fill the top of our sales funnel. That hasn't changed. What has changed is that many times buyers will position themselves at the top of the funnel by searching for goods and services online and finding our companies.

The '*"Willing To Buy"* Framework' answers the question. *"Okay…what's next?"*. On your first conversation with this new breed of buyers, it is important to begin the process of separating the motivated and qualified buyers from the tire kickers, the gate keepers from the decision makers. The tools inherent to the '*"Willing To Buy"* Framework' provide the tried and true and ultimately most economical way to disqualify.

Yes, again I said disqualify. Sales people are expensive. Sales calls are expensive. Developing a well written proposal is expensive. The quicker we get to the core of who will buy, why they are buying, whether they can afford to buy and the consequences of not buying, the quicker we can focus our time on the right buyers, those truly '*"Willing To Buy"*'.

So yes, certainly "things have changed". As managers, we also need to change. We need to focus our attention on adding clarity to the sales process. We need to eliminate "hopium" wherever it exists and dig out the reality of each and every deal. While we appreciate and make use of all the new tools and technologies now available one fact remains. Successful salespeople know what wins deals. It's the "people stuff". The '"*Willing To Buy*" Framework' focuses on that unchanging truth.

Printed in the United States
By Bookmasters